Meet Like You Mean It - a Leader's Guide to Painless and Productive Virtual Meetings

Wayne Turmel

Published by Achis Marketing Services
5946 Greenview Rd
Lisle, IL 60532
www.GreatWebMeetings.com
Join us on Twitter @greatwebmeeting
Google + greatwebmeetings.com
ISBN 978-0-9820377-3-7

DEDICATION

This book is for The Duchess and Her Serene Highness. Whenever I endure a lousy meeting, I remember why and put down the sharp objects and breathe.

Table of Contents

Introduction

How to Get the Most from This Book

This book is for leaders. Not necessarily "Senior Leaders" with titles, but those of us who are leading the way at work: managers, individual supervisors and project managers. We're just out there trying to get our work done as best we can with not nearly enough resources and assistance.

If you've found yourself having to lead webinars or virtual meetings, with no training, coaching or guidance, you're in the right place.

There are two types of readers for this book. The first will start at the beginning and work through it methodically. Your mother would be proud.

We firmly believe that context is important. The tips and practices we suggest are based on your work being improved by making webmeetings more painless and productive. In order to do that we think it's important that we understand why they're not that way, exactly what's wrong, and what we can do about it right now.

We're confident you'll find the time well invested, and it's not like it's War and Peace. It's an easy read.

The second group of readers will look at the table of contents and "skip to the good stuff". It's okay, we're not hurt. In fact, we've made it easy for you by drawing your attention to the best practices and tips by prominently marking the best practices with an icon like this

Go on. Skip to the tips, although I'd suggest you start with Section 2, "About the Technology". After all, 80% of users use only 25% of the available features on most webmeeting and collaboration platforms, so there's your low hanging fruit. Go on...you're excused. Get outa here. Don't let the title page give you a paper cut on the way out.

Now, where were we?

We're confident you'll find enough ways to make your virtual meetings more productive and painless that it will be well worth the investment in time and effort.

How can you make the best use of your time? Some of you will read through the book cover to cover. Then you'll go back to the pages you highlighted, dog-eared, sticky noted or otherwise marked, (depending on the format of the book) and apply the tips. That's great. Have at it.

Other people will read until they find something worth trying, go play with it, and then come back. In a way, that's actually the best approach. When it comes to technology, the best time to explore, play, and apply is when you are curious about a topic, but there's no pressure. The time to try out the whiteboard on your Lync platform is not when your boss is looking on.

We've designed this book to be skimmed, sampled and used roughly. Copy the worksheets, or visit www.GreatWebMeetings.com/resources/meetlikeyoumeanit and download fresh PDF copies of the 'Meet Like You Mean It Worksheets" so you can use them over and over. Put the book down and come back to it when you get frustrated or need fresh ideas.

Just as an aside, one of the things you'll notice about this book is we're platform neutral. There are plenty of tools and tech designed to help you plan, present and conduct great meetings. Some are primarily presentation platforms with great meeting and collaboration tools (Adobe Connect, WebEx, GoToMeeting and dozens of others) and some are specifically designed to help you with meetings (LucidMeeting, LessMeeting, Microsoft Lync and who knows how many others). If you find a tool you and your team can work with, great. If you are handed a tool by the nice folks in IT and told this is what you have, make that work too.

You'll also get something that's unique to this book. Using many of the tools and techniques we use at GreatWebMeetings.com with our customers around the world, you'll have a chance to assess the way your in-person and online meetings run now.

The purpose of this book is to help make virtual meetings less painful for both managers and managed. By the end of our time together you'll know how to:

- Uncover the tools at your disposal and understand how to use them in the context of a productive meeting
- Invest time planning to make your meetings more efficient
- Plan the meeting to achieve your desired outcome
- Get the best possible input so you get the best possible output
- Lead the meeting, don't just run it (and there's a huge difference)
- Manage time and stay on track

If you're going to invest the time, money and mental capital to hold or attend a meeting, you should meet like you mean it.

Section: 1

Virtual Meetings Suck, and Why That Matters

"If I have a choice between attending a meeting and a dirty nappy, I'll choose the nappy."

Film director, Tim Burton

In the nearly 20 years I've been in management and training, I've talked with people at companies all over the world about what make managers crazy. Oh sure, there are the usual suspects: number-based performance reviews, bosses that don't ask before implementing policies, IT people who don't understand the word "broken" and insist on more detail…but by far, the number one crankiness-inducing thing in our lives is meetings.

Is this distaste irrational? Do we really hate meetings that much? If so, why do we have so many of them?

Boy, do we hold a lot of meetings. And a growing number of them are happening virtually.

- According to multiple studies, managers spend at least 50% of their time in meetings. Assuming an 8-hour workday (quit laughing…we need a number to work with), this means we spend at least 1,100 hours a year in meetings, whether in person or through technology.

- In 2013 there were over 22 million web meetings held—about 15 million via WebEx. You know that number hasn't gone down a bit since then.

We're spending an increasing amount of our lives holding meetings that happen through technology. WebEx, Microsoft Lync, Adobe Connect, GoToMeeting…at last count there are over 120 web meeting, webinar or collaboration tools out there.

With so many tools at our disposal, you'd think any problems we have with webmeetings or virtual meetings (the two are interchangeable, at least for the moment) would be easily solved. But let's take a look at some terrifying, or at least depressing, statistics:

- If we use the 22 million number, and each meeting lasts one hour, American businesses spend about 22 million hours in virtual meetings. Let's assume each meeting has an average of 3 people in it. That's 66 million person-hours per year.

- According to multiple studies, participants in those meetings consider a minimum of 2/3 of the time spent in webmeetings a "waste of time". That means about 44 million online hours down the tubes. Multiply those hours by the wages of the people on the call, and you have hundreds of millions of dollars flushed away.

- Look at your personal numbers. If you spend 1,100 hours in meetings, and half of those are virtual, that's 550 hours spent in online communication. If 2/3 of that time is wasted, that's 366 hours of your life you'll never get back. That's roughly 9 weeks of your year.

Think about those numbers for a moment. If you were doing anything else at work that had a 70% failure rate, with that kind of money and time attached, how long would you and your company tolerate it? The Six-Sigma black belts among us would have a field day.

Part of the problem, I suspect, is how we think about meetings.

I remember being in a meeting that lasted half a day. I was still new and had a younger man's stamina then. I was trying my best to listen, contribute and be a good team member. (Take a good look at your interns. They're so cute at that age.) When the meeting was over, the leader stood up and said, "Okay, let's get back to work". I remember thinking, "What the #@%$@%$ have I been doing for the last four hours?" The meeting, necessary and productive as it was, was seen as separate from the work of the team.

Here's the key question that bubbled up in my mind and has nagged me in the years since: *If the main purpose of our having a job is to get work done, and the meetings aren't part of that work, exactly why do we have them?*

The answer, of course, is that in a righteous universe, meetings are designed to help us get the work done. We need information to make things work. Good decisions need to be made. Stakeholders need to talk to one another so we're not toiling in a vacuum. Constructive discussion and even arguments need to occur in a structured environment. Human beings need to create the kind of positive relationships that lead to trust, honesty, pulling in the same direction and being willing to go out of our way for each other. For many of us, working with other people actually allows us to have fun and enjoy what we do.

The fact that they're virtual is simply a function of the fact that we no longer work in the same locations as our teammates. If we are to meet productively, much of that will have to be done online.

The reasons to hold meetings certainly don't change whether they're through Lync or held in the third floor conference room. Here are 10 purposes for a meeting. I'm sure you can think of more:

1. Share information between participants that drives the work forward

2. Create social interaction

3. Hold brain storming sessions

4. Solve problems

5. Give context to your individual work

6. Reward and recognize both individual and team accomplishments

7. Identify issues the team needs to be aware of to avoid major problems later

8. Express different viewpoints in a controlled manner

9. Get real-time (and just-in-time) input from disparate sources and process that information

10. Answer any questions so everyone gets the same answers in the same way

We should probably add "have fun" to the mix because we are essentially social creatures (most of us, at least--my apologies to the terminally introverted). Social interaction is a by-product of most meetings, and it's vitally important; but it seldom makes the list of reasons because, darn it, this is work and should be taken seriously.

After scanning the list, there's a logical conclusion to be reached. We meet because there's no other way to share information and make decisions critical to our jobs that's nearly as effective. If form follows function, then a good meeting in any form is one that allows a focused, honest, constructive flow of high-quality information that drives the work forward. People are heard, information is gathered and digested, decisions are made and we move on. Possibly they're fun, or at least not bottomless pits of misery.

In fact, as more and more of us work separately from our teammates, virtual meetings actually become more important--not less.

That's not to say that technology alone is the answer to bad meetings. In fact, there are two related pieces of information I have always kept in mind:

1. Genghis Khan ruled half the known world very effectively and never held a WebEx meeting. Now, I'm not suggesting you use his methods of accountability and performance review (although they were effective, even if HR wouldn't approve.) The point is, when a team is properly motivated, aligned and held accountable it's easier to handle the whole time-and-distance problem.

2. Having great tools doesn't mean that the meetings will be any better. It's what you do with them. Just as in the old movie "Soylent Green", the secret ingredient is people. A well-led, inspired team with lousy tools will beat the heck out of a lousy team with a great IT budget almost every time.

Human beings have never had to meet the way we do now. We encounter circumstances that are unique to webmeetings, and most of us have never received much guidance. In fact, 75% or more of people who use only presentation tools receive no training before they are expected to use them.

We have online meetings run by people who haven't been well trained to run regular meetings, using technology they also haven't been properly trained on working with people who aren't sure how to use the tool themselves and don't want to be there in the first place. Why is it any surprise that most people use their time online to catch up on email?

Other than marriage, I can't think of another thing that takes up so much of our lives and we're supposed to learn solely from example, history and our guts.

But misery there is…by the bucket load.

You don't need statistics to tell you what's wrong with most meetings, but here are some anyway. According to studies, here's why we hate meetings:

It doesn't seem to matter if we're the leader or merely an innocent by-stander, here's an unscientific look at what we're doing during these same meetings:

HOW WE SPEND OUR TIME IN BAD MEETINGS

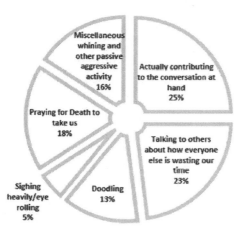

These behaviors, of course, are not terribly productive and are even worse if it's your meeting to run.

Here, in no particular order are some of the most common complaints about meetings. If you've already done the assessment you may seem that some, or many, of them apply to the meetings you attend:

- People show up in a bad mood, reluctant to be there and already planning their escape.

- Meetings take too long (sometimes because they start late, sometimes they end late and too often it just feels like it shouldn't take so long).

- Meetings get off track.

- People aren't properly prepared so there's either too much redundancy or you run out of time (which results in frustration and more meetings).

- The same people talk over and over…and the same people never say a word or contribute.

- People don't do what they commit to doing, which basically negates all the hard work done in the meeting and can damage the ongoing working relationships.

- The meeting leader doesn't appear to be in control.

- The outcomes of the meeting don't make up for the other things you could be doing which results in frustration (which means people show up for the next meeting in a bad mood, reluctant to be there…and lather, rinse, repeat.).

These are timeless, traditional, meeting challenges. Odds are not much has changed since King Arthur put in that round table so he could actually see what was happening around him and what that weasel Bedivere was up to.

In the virtual world, of course, there are additional problems that are unique to that environment:

1. People don't participate. The more suspicious meeting leaders suspect they've put the phone on mute and are just answering email.

2. They really are just putting the phone on mute and answering email.

3. The technology is more of a hassle than it's worth, so many of the features of these collaboration and web presentation tools go unused.

4. The meeting leader is so stressed by the technology that it interferes with the listening, questioning and facilitating that makes a meeting work.

5. We spend a lot of time emailing people documents they should already have (like the latest version of whatever you're working on).

6. You spend a lot of time re-sending meeting invitations and other logistical information, then waiting too long for people to connect.

7. People treat virtual meetings like they're not real, and don't take them as seriously as in-person meetings.

So let's assume for a moment that you actually want to fix these problems. You want to get a piece of your life back, and get results at the same time. Here's how we'll do it:

- We're going to identify the problems that are specific to your team meetings. This will mean asking yourself some hard questions.

- We'll assume you'll actually DO the things we talk about.

- You're going to USE the tools included in this book to change your behavior—both as a meeting leader and a participant.

- You will IGNORE the taunts of the other kids who will threaten to beat you up after school and take your lunch money. (Yes, workplace dynamics look a lot like middle school.) If it helps any, you were never one of the cool kids to start with and your mother is right, they're just jealous of you.

Let's start by taking a look at what people do during your meetings now. What's working and what isn't? One of these assessments is for face-to-face gatherings, the other is for your virtual meetings.

You're smart people so you'll see right away that the two are almost the same. Almost; but not quite.

In our research with hundreds of people who have attended both in-person meetings and online sessions, the differences between them are small but significant, rather than major differences in content or intent.

For example, in person meetings often start later and run longer than conference calls or webmeetings. This is partly because of the social component of being in actual contact with other human beings. It's also because we seem biologically incapable of judging how long it will take us to actually leave what we're doing and navigate to the conference room.

On the other hand, there's a fear that people are not really paying attention on webmeetings, that they're answering email or putting you on mute while they do something they consider more important. Anyone who's ever received an email from someone they were on the phone with understands how this works. If you've sent such an email, you're guilty. Anyone who has actually read it during the meeting is complicit.

You know who you are.

Let's ask you some basic questions to assess your current meetings. The tools are pretty self-explanatory:

Traditional Meeting Assessment Checklist

Meeting Factor	Meets/Doesn't Meet Expectations (be specific)	Next Steps (be specific)
The meetings start on time		
The desired outcome is clearly stated at the start of each meeting		
The meetings have a detailed agenda		
Participants received the agenda in plenty of time to prepare for the meeting		
All participants have all necessary documents or information before discussion starts		
All participants clearly understand the rules for taking questions, feedback and comments		
The most important action items are handled first		
Sufficient tools like clean whiteboards, handouts and chart paper are available		
The session leader appears in control of the participants		
All participants are solicited for input		

All participants' opinions are heard and respected		
Questions are solicited and answered to the participants' satisfaction		
All action items are clearly recapped and documented		
The objectives are met and next steps are clear		
The meeting stays on track and (more or less) on time		

Virtual Meeting Assessment Checklist

Meeting Factor	Meets/Doesn't Meet Expectations (be specific)	Next Steps (be specific)
The meetings start on time		
The desired outcome is clearly stated at the start of each meeting		
The meetings have a detailed agenda		
Participants receive the agenda in plenty of time to prepare for the meeting		
All participants have all necessary documents or information before discussion starts		

All participants clearly understand the rules for taking questions, feedback and comments		
The most important action items are handled first		
The session leader appears in control of the technology		
The session leader appears in control of the interaction and discussion		
All participants are solicited for input		
All participants' opinions are heard and respected		
Questions are solicited and answered to the participants' satisfaction		
The technology functions properly (e.g., people can join the meeting with little problem or drama)		
The technology actually adds value to the process, and isn't a distraction		
All action items are clearly recapped and documented		
The objectives are met and next steps are clear		
The meeting stays on track and (more or less) on time		

Take a moment to look over your results. A couple of things should leap out to you:

- The results probably aren't surprising. Most sentient beings understand in their guts what's wrong with their meetings. It's all out in the open now. You have no excuses for ignoring it.

- The criteria for success between virtual and traditional meetings are actually very similar. The purpose, objectives and desired behaviors (participation, good thinking, achieved objectives, and playing nicely with others) are identical. The difference is that they are mediated by technology which makes them an order of magnitude more difficult. Learn to deal with the technology, then the skills required from both participants and meeting leaders are almost identical no matter how the meeting is held.

Let's start by looking at the biggest difference between traditional and online meetings. It's also the one most people are stressed about: the technology.

Section 2:

Virtual Meeting Tools and Tech

"One machine can do the work of 50 ordinary men. No machine can do the work of one extraordinary man."

American writer and hopeless optimist Elbert Hubbard

The Elephant in the (Virtual Meeting) Room

Odds are, that this section is the main reason you're reading this book. In fact, you may have skipped everything and flipped right to this section. If so, welcome.

Study after study shows that the technology is the biggest concern of both meeting leaders and attendees. Will it work? Can I handle the distractions? How will we communicate if I can't see the people I'm speaking to, and they can't see me?

We need to take a second to remember several things we said in the introduction:

- Meetings take place in the context of work, and to drive the work forward. That hasn't changed.

- The technology is only a tool to help us achieve what always had to happen anyway. It can be done without technology, it's just easier with the right tools. (See the Romans, Mongols, British Empire and any other dispersed working group throughout history.)

- It's not like our face-to-face meetings were some kind of golden age of efficiency and great time management.

Technology, then, is a constraint--maybe even a complicating factor--but it is not a deal breaker. At least it doesn't have to be. At GreatWebMeetings.com we believe there are only three key factors about using technology at work we really need to consider:

1. The goals of meetings, virtual or otherwise, are to share information, build working relationships and drive the work forward.

2. Technology allows us to bridge gaps in communication caused by working remotely…

3. …Only if we understand what the technology can (and can't) do, and use it appropriately and optimally.

In this section, we're going to take a look at the tools most common webmeeting and presentation platforms share. We'll examine a lot of features, but only in the context of how they help share information, generate input and drive your work towards completion.

We also are platform neutral. We don't care what you use. WebEx, Adobe Connect, Microsoft Lync, smoke signals and cave drawings, all will work if you use them properly and in context. None of them will work if you aren't really interested in making them work.

This technology is constantly changing. The last competitive analysis I saw suggested there are over 120 webmeeting/ presentation/collaboration platforms out there. The good news is they all do about 90% of the same things.

All we ask is that as you explore each tool at your disposal, you ask yourself a couple of simple questions:

- Do I know if my platform has a similar tool, and do I know where to find it?

- Will it help me and my teams hold more successful meetings and get our work done?

- Can I use it with any kind of confidence or competence?

At the end of the day, these are tips and suggestions. We are sure you'll find them helpful, but none of them will matter if you don't develop the muscle memory and comfort with them to make smart decisions. Whether you use a whiteboard or not should be determined by whether it will help you get your work done better, not by whether you worry you can't type and listen at the same time.

In this section we've broken down the most common features of webmeeting platforms, given you some examples of how to use them, and identified some best practices you can apply immediately.

When you find something of interest, put the book down (or just close the window, depending on how you're reading this), go to your platform and poke around. There's really no other way to learn.

It will take time, but you'll be surprised at how many features and tools these platforms have, and how they can make your meetings more robust, interesting and productive. You'll also learn the features that are cool, but don't add any value. Great. The trick is to make conscious decisions about what to use and when.

Once we get past the concern about the technology, we'll be able to focus better on what it takes to lead great virtual meetings.

Have at it.

Permissions and Who Can Do What

Think about really good team meetings you've attended. The meeting leader doesn't do everything, do they? Surely you don't have to present, hook up the computer, hand out copies, write on the board, take notes for the participants, serve the doughnuts and pour the coffee. (I'm assuming. If you are doing all those things, you need to think seriously about your delegation skills).

Instead, you ask for help. More likely, the folks around the table voluntarily take on these piddling little tasks so the meeting doesn't get bogged down and they can help you, and each other, out. Those little interactions can tell you a lot about the group. Are they willing to lend a hand? Are they proactive or passive? Do they look like they even care?

You'll notice as we tour the various features of webmeetings the tools that make it easy to replicate, maybe even improve on, the in-room, traditional meeting experience. If you want to make the information you and your folks present easily available and easy to use, you want to think about the various ways to use the tool in as collaborative a fashion as possible.

This starts with setting permissions; what people are allowed to do and banned from doing.

Why you want to use this tool

I've come to believe that the people who design webmeeting tools might be anti-social control freaks. I certainly apologize if I'm wrong, but the default settings for interaction tend to limit how people share information and interact.

Think about a traditional meeting. People can speak up, move to the front of the room to help out with the whiteboard, get access to handouts in the moment…there's a lot going on. If people want to help each other out, they can.

By setting permissions to allow meeting attendees maximum control, you not only replicate that real-life example, but you can even surpass it by allowing people to print just in time. They can prepare their contributions to the meeting while other work gets done.

For our purposes we won't worry about specific platforms, just functions. You can play around and discover where they are on the platform you use.

Meeting Setup Permissions

Have you ever been scheduled for a webmeeting and shown up on time only to be kept in the "lobby" until it officially starts? Basically this means starting at a blank, mute screen until the meeting leader shows up and pushes the "start" button.

It's a lot like showing up at a face-to-face meeting, only to be kept standing in the hallway until the leader unlocks the door.

This is less than optimal for a few reasons:

- It's frustrating to show up on time and be kept waiting

- Everyone joins at the same time, and there's chaos while people say hello, log in, and generally talk over each other

- Everyone is troubleshooting their technical problems at the same time

- If the meeting leader is late, nothing else can be done and nobody else can take charge until he or she gets there

Now think about what happens in most other meetings. People show up a little early and there are side conversations. They pick out their seats and get organized. They rush off and get copies or pick up what they've forgotten.

All this activity not only creates social interaction and builds relationships, (chatting and making nice is part of your job, despite what some engineer-types will tell you) but it also means once the meeting actually starts there's less stress and you can get down to business quicker.

Now imagine a virtual meeting where people can chat with each other casually and troubleshoot technical problems before everyone else has to wait for them. If you have multiple presenters, they can each prepare for their segment by uploading files and preparing whiteboards and polls in advance. If someone needs a document, they can simply click a button and print it out right from the meeting or download it to somewhere useful on their computer (rather than to their email, which they'll lose or delete).

Set everyone up as a speaker or panelist

The language varies from platform to platform, but if you want people to contribute as equals, they should have equal access to the platform. You wouldn't expect people in a live meeting to sit unproductively waiting for you, why allow that in your online meetings? Allow everyone to join early, upload anything they want to present in advance of their turn.

Here's what it looks like in Microsoft Lync:

×

Lync Meeting Options

CONVERSATION

These people don't have to wait in the lobby:

| Anyone (no restrictions) ▼ | Why do I use this?

☐ Announce when people enter or leave

Who's a presenter?

| Anyone (no restrictions) ▼ |

Presenters can share content and let people into the meeting.

Who can annotate PowerPoint presentations?

| Presenters only ▼ |

Who can look at content on their own?

| Presenters only ▼ | When is a good time to use this?

This lets people browse a separate copy of what's being presented without affecting what everyone else is seeing.

| OK | | Cancel |

Decide in advance what you want them to do during the meeting.

Before your session even starts, you have to decide what permissions people will have based on what you want to happen during the meeting. Here's what you can allow your meeting participants to do in WebEx:

 The fewer participants, the more democratic you want to be about the permissions. If you have a large town-hall type meeting, you might want to limit the ability for all 200 people to write in the chat, just to maintain your sanity and maintain order. This is especially true if the topic of the meeting will be emotional. You can still allow them to send chat messages, comments or questions to the meeting leader and their assistant(s) and receive written responses or you can address them verbally.

Don't let paranoia get the best of you

In general, I tend to allow everything. First, I trust my people not to abuse the privilege (although they do have a disturbing tendency to use the drawing tools to put horns on my picture). Secondly, it's easier for me to set the meeting settings by default and leave them be. It's one less thing I have to do once the meeting starts.

 If you have proprietary information that can't leave your company, take that into account when setting permissions. Rather than use file transfer for. Power Point files, for example, simply allow saving uploaded files as PDFs which will not display speaker's notes. Or don't allow people to save directly from the meeting except through file transfer where you can control what leaves the building. Of course, the really enterprising participants will just use a screen capture tool like Snagit, so how much control do you really have anyway?

Letting people print documents and such is also helpful if you want to "go green" or if they are under 30 and don't know exactly what paper is for.

The Whiteboard Feature

One of the most useful features of webmeeting tools is also one of the most under-utilized—the whiteboard. There are numerous ways to use a whiteboard that not only captures information, but gets people kinesthetically involved. It allows everyone to contribute and be engaged, creates a permanent record, and you can share that information to ensure consistency, accuracy and reference for later.

Truthfully, most people use whiteboards simply to capture information just like they would in a traditional meeting, but they can be so much more and add so much more value. How so?

Why you want to use this tool

The most obvious way to use a whiteboard is to treat it like…well, like a traditional whiteboard or flipchart. How do you use a whiteboard or flipchart in a traditional meeting setting?

Maybe you use it to generate discussion. Maybe you're creating a "parking lot" of issues to be discussed later so you don't get off track. That's great, and the whiteboard feature will do all of that in a simple (with a little practice) way. But it can do so much more.

People love the spontaneity of it. To be cynical, there's "something happening" visually on the screen which captures your audience's attention. Using a whiteboard to generate ideas or input creates an opportunity for feedback and great thinking as you call for more information. It gets people working on a verbal and vocal, as well as a visual, level.

You can have as many whiteboards as you want

Have you ever been in a meeting and run out of whiteboard space? Or flipchart paper? Have you desperately searched for tape or pins or a place to hang a sheet of paper so you can move on to the next one? This is never a problem in a virtual meeting (and you don't have to ask the nice lady in facilities for one of her precious easel stands or markers that actually work either).

Most platforms allow you to create as many whiteboards as you need. Let's say you want to keep a running "parking lot" of issues to be discussed later. You might not be using that screen at the moment, but may have to flip back to it at any time. By having a dedicated whiteboard you can move easily from a presentation to the whiteboard in question, write down the item and return with the push of a tab or file name (depending on the platform). With only a little practice this becomes second nature. But it does take the practice to get used to it. Until then it's like rubbing your head and patting your stomach, but a far more useful skill.

Let's assume you're doing some brainstorming, so you want a blank whiteboard solely for that purpose. You can create a workspace in the moment (usually by doing something complicated like pushing a button marked "create new whiteboard").

BEST PRACTICE: One great way to have a smooth meeting is to prepare and upload your whiteboards in advance. This not only shows good planning on your part, but reduces busywork during the meeting itself. It also looks kind of cool.

For example, you can create a simple "fishbone" diagram for problem solving in about seven strokes of your mouse using the line-drawing tools available on most whiteboards. When you get to that part of the agenda, you're ready to rock and roll.

BEST PRACTICE: Re-name the whiteboards as you create them. By default, most new whiteboards are numbered, so you have "whiteboard 1", "whiteboard 2", and so on If you name them as you go, you'll make it easy to navigate and flip from one to the other.

In WebEx you can do this by having either the session host or the presenter right click on the tab for that whiteboard, click "rename" and call it whatever you want. In Microsoft Lync, you can go to the Shared Content list, right click on the whiteboard in question and call it whatever you desire.

Save whiteboards for future reference--or better yet, let people download them to their own computer instantly.

Have you ever been in a really productive idea-generating meeting and had multiple pages of chart paper spread all over the room? Or maybe you're holding multiple meetings and wind up having to unwrinkle sheets from the last session to pick up where you left off?

In order to turn that into useful information, one poor soul (probably you or some hapless intern) has to take them, save them, make sense of them after the fact, transcribe them to something like a Word document, then email it out to all meeting participants and anyone else who cares.

It's a pain for the person who takes on this task. It also causes delays, transcription errors and semi-legitimate excuses for "not getting the list of action items". Take the onus off someone else and make everyone else responsible by allowing (and then insisting and holding accountable) everyone to save the whiteboards and other documents in real time, on their own devices, in whatever place makes sense to them.

You can do this by setting permissions before the meeting even starts (see the chapter on Meeting Permissions). Set the session so that all participants can save and print documents directly from the meeting.

Allow everyone (or at least one other person) permission to write on the board

As we've already discussed, the multitasking involved in leading a meeting and using the technology at the same time is a major reason people don't use tools like this effectively, if at all. I've looked, there is no federal law stating you must do everything yourself.

Designate an assistant or consider letting everyone write their own ideas on the whiteboard. Not only does this free you up for better things, but it forces the easily-distracted to stay connected to the meeting and get physically involved, rather than stay passive. Be aware that if you let everyone type on their own you will experience a lag and it will be messy as people write over each other. Some platforms, like Adobe Connect, let you drag and drop text and move it around, some don't. It depends on your tolerance for chaos.

You're probably not shocked to discover this doesn't bother me much, but it drives engineering/very linear types crazy.

BEST PRACTICE: In order to prevent people scribbling all over your carefully compiled list of action items, take the time at the beginning of the meeting to teach people proper use of the tools and set ground rules for their use.

Use annotation tools to generate feedback

Besides allowing people to write text on the screen, most platforms have a lot of ways people can contribute. This is really useful for getting feedback from the audience. Let's say you've generated a list of action items and you need to reach consensus on how to move forward. By using check marks, or X's you can allow people to vote in real time. This not only forces everyone to participate, you can do things on the fly without the formality and complication of using Polling or other features.

Here's what it looks like in WebEx:

Ways to Save the Johnson Account

LinkedIn connections√
Attend trade shows √√ √
More cold calls√
Offer new products (version 2.0) √
Switch account reps√

BEST PRACTICE: Have everyone choose a color for their annotations, and stick to it as much as possible. This will reduce confusion during meetings, if you know that Mark's annotations are green and Rajesh is usually blue.

It's worth investing some time at the beginning of your meeting (especially if it's the first time this group has met or people aren't familiar with the tools) to let them know what annotation tools are available and how to use them. It will dramatically increase the odds of them being utilized.

The whiteboard can come in handy for team building exercises

Whiteboards are great for informal or spontaneous presentations. Didn't plan a PowerPoint slide for a certain point? Go to the board. Someone doesn't have an online profile everyone can check out? Make one on the fly.

One of my favorite features, and not every platform allows for it, is the ability to cut and paste pictures and images on a whiteboard. (Microsoft Lync does, WebEx, not so much). This makes it easy to share photos which can go a long way to creating human connections. When people introduce themselves, have them share a photograph with the team (I like to use photos that are candid but not incriminating).

The picture I use most is me posing with the Stanley Cup. It says, "I'm Canadian, I'm a hockey fan, and I had twenty bucks that day". It also is a great conversation starter and will make you a rock star with people from the Czech Republic and Slovakia. Really.

While using the board as directed is optimal, there's usually a work-around

In some platforms, like many of the Citrix products (GoToMeeting, GoToWebinar, etc.), ReadyTalk and others that simply share screens, the whiteboards are either nonexistent or not particularly easy to use. There are options:

- Open a Word document and simply use that (or several of them) in place of a whiteboard. They are easy to save and share.

- If you aren't able to share pictures and images on the whiteboard, as in WebEx, you can upload the picture as a file and simply annotate on the picture itself. This is great for technical diagrams and maps.

Go play with your platform's whiteboard features soon. Figure out what it can do, and ask yourself: how can this help us meet more effectively?

Attachments and File Transfer

Good meetings rely on the easy and quick exchange of information, and a lot of that information takes the form of documents. In a traditional meeting, we'd think of these as handouts—copies of the visuals, articles to review, or spreadsheets to dive into and examine. In virtual meetings these are equally important but you don't have an intern running around the table throwing piles of paper into everyone's laps.

You can get around this by using a function that, depending on platform, is either called "file transfer" or "attachments".

Why you want to use these tools

Managing documents, visuals and handouts in meetings can be a pain. People flip ahead until you're ready to discuss certain topics. They get lost in minutiae and take the meeting off track. You have to take time to pass out the papers during the meeting which can be a bit of a distraction.

Additionally, we've all had those meetings where you are about to get into the topic at hand, only to have someone say, "I didn't get that attachment, can someone send it to me?" Then there's a delay while you go out of the meeting screen to your email, resend it (assuming you can find it yourself in a hurry and it's not too big a file to squeeze through your email) and wait for the little "ding" that says they've received it in their email. There has to be a better way.

There is.

Most platforms either allow for simple file transfer or allow you to attach documents through your meeting platform.

Why they're better than email

Most people use their email really poorly. They download attachments and can't remember where they are when they need them. They move documents to files that may or may not allow easy access when they need the documents. Frequently they delete emails, attachments and all, before they're even read.

Additionally, folks have to leave the meeting software in order to access the information. Any excuse to wander off will probably mean you've lost them for a time. Also, sending them to their email gives them tacit permission to pay attention to their email…which we all know is a major distraction.

Nowadays, people may be attending your virtual meeting on a tablet or a smartphone, in which case the document they downloaded and printed may not even be available when they need to refer to it.

By using the file transfer or attachment tool, when people say "I don't have that, can you resend it?" you can say no, but with one click you can download it right to your computer.

Here's what it looks like in WebEx:

And here's what it looks like in Lync 2013. Earlier versions may differ, but you're looking for the paperclip symbol:

It's nice to share…especially extra, unexpected information

How often have you been in a meeting and someone mentions an article they read, or a document they got from someone else? People say "Hey, can you send me a copy of that?" This is a good thing--you want people to share information. It could add value to the meeting, and it builds good bonds between co-workers. Voluntarily sharing information is a good sign that you're engaged and care about the team.

Maybe the information is critical and you need it NOW. By allowing everyone access to the file transfer or to upload attachments, they can do it without even leaving the meeting. If they have to search for it, they can do so while the team takes care of its current business.

Now, some people will be really interested, and take the time to download print and even (heaven forbid!) read the new article. Others will not care, or delete it without reading. File transfer allows you to choose what you download and where it goes. The sender doesn't have to remember who wanted it and who didn't, if someone cares, they can download it without wasting everyone's time.

You control when they have access to files

If you've ever tried to lead a discussion or make a presentation while people (usually senior management) flip through your handouts, you know it can be a huge distraction to both the audience and yourself. How cool would it be if you could give them the presentation when you're good and ready?

By controlling what's available for download when, usually with the single click of a mouse, you can make documents available just in time, rather than have everyone download them and be distracted.

If something is for later reference, make it available later. If you're doing a presentation that has some element of surprise, keep the PowerPoint file available after the fact. I like to make read-only PDF copies of my visuals available (people always ask for them but they don't contain my notes like the PPT files would) and offer them as downloads at the end of customer meetings or webinars. Those who want them have access, and those who don't aren't getting more useless, immediately deleted emails or printed copies that just kill trees and waste paper.

 BEST PRACTICE: Decide beforehand when you want people to get the documents you're sharing. In WebEx, for example, you can upload everything in advance and simply check the appropriate boxes for files to be available. Keep the box unchecked until you're ready for everyone to get the information, then check it and tell they to download it at will.

Yet another reason to allow everyone access.

If it sounds like all of this can involve multi-tasking, you're not wrong. By setting your permissions for others to have access to the file transfer function, you can say, "Kelly, would you attach that for everyone while we continue?" Then you don't have to stop what you're doing for what is, after all, an administrative task.

Also, by allowing everyone access, you increase the chances of spontaneous sharing of information which is something you really want if your team is going to be creative and productive.

Uploading Files, Application and Screen Sharing

One of the most common ways to use webmeeting platforms is to share your screen. Want to show a PowerPoint presentation? Great. Working on a spreadsheet with your team? Terrific. What's interesting is that most people, even (maybe especially) those who've been using these tools the longest, are doing it wrong and missing out on a way to get the most out of any virtual meeting.

The fact is that most of the time, you're better off uploading your presentation, documents or other files to the platform's server, rather than simply sharing your screen. There are several reasons for this:

- Screen speed: Sharing files is faster than sharing applications, which is faster than sharing your whole desktop.

- Privacy: If you're sharing your desktop, the audience will see everything that happens on your computer. This includes email announcements, virus blocker popups, or even instant messages asking, "Are you still on that lame meeting?" (True story, and it left a scar.)

- Ease of passing control: If a document is loaded to the server, anyone can take control and present. If you can only show what's on your screen, it's awkward to change presenters smoothly.

- Maximizing all the other tools webmeetings provide: If you're showing your visuals in the "stage" area, you have room on the screen to monitor the chat, use your webcam, annotate and easily navigate from your presentation to your whiteboards, to polls and back again.

All of this, by the way, assumes that the platform you're using allows you to upload presentations, documents and files in advance. My experience has been that the Citrix platforms like GoToMeeting, GoToWebinar etc. are built differently and only allow you to share and present from your computer .

Here's what you should see when running a meeting in WebEx. Notice that you can follow the chat, what the participants are up to and have access to annotation tools while showing your visuals to best effect.

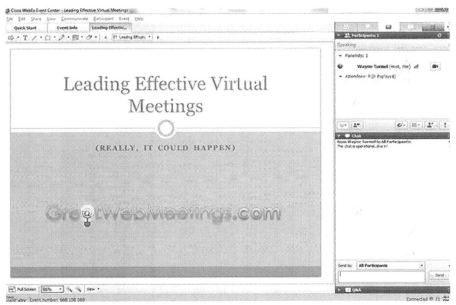

Why you want to use these tools

Most of this section will presume you're working with visuals you've uploaded in advance. When should you upload your visuals and when should you just share your screen?

Share your screen when:

- Time is of the essence. If you are meeting and suddenly get the idea to show what you're talking about or you want someone else to show you what they're looking at on their screen, then go ahead. Just click "share desktop" and have at it. Also just do this when there's nothing else you'll be doing in the meeting.

- If you're showing an application or website where you'll be doing a lot of navigation or showing a number of applications off the same computer. If you're showing a series of live applications, and that's the primary goal of your meeting, have at it.

- Firewall or security issues make uploading files difficult. This is a great work-around if you're having problems with the platform as it's designed. This usually isn't a problem if everyone on your meeting is on the same network or work for the same company. Sometimes, though, you will experience a problem. This happens a lot with systems that are primarily designed for internal use like Microsoft Lync. (For the record, it's usually a Port problem, but unless you are in IT that won't mean much to you and there's not much you can do about it once your meeting starts).

 BEST PRACTICE: If you absolutely must share your screen, do yourself a big favor and close all other applications, especially those that suddenly pop into action like email and instant messaging. Seriously. If it happens on your computer, your audience will see it.

Also, remember that this is the slowest option in terms of response. Think of your web connection as a pipe. When you share your desktop, you're sharing all the data running around on your computer, whether your audience sees it or not.

Share only the application or program when:

- Collaboration requires that you work on documents in real time. The opportunity for several people to work together on a single document is the single best reason to share a program or application. People can do their own work, if that helps. It allows you to have a single, definitive version of a document and save it in real time.

- When training, do you want them to know what to do—or demonstrate they can do it? So often in meetings we need to teach our team to do something. Let's say that you're teaching them to place an order in the new software. You can show a whole series of screen shots, or have everyone sit back passively and watch…but if you really want to know someone can do something, give them control and make them prove it. Not to be cynical, but just the threat of having to demonstrate competence will make them pay attention, so there's that.

- You are only sharing one program or website during your meeting. If you are only sharing one program during your meeting, simply share that program or application. One big advantage is that the program will only show that application or program and everything else running will be invisible. You won't have any embarrassing popups.

- Your program doesn't support animation in PowerPoint, and they're important to your presentation. Most programs are built knowing that PowerPoint is the standard (work of the devil or not, it IS the most common presentation tool out there. Live with it.) and are designed to work well with it.

- You have to show an application or website as well as navigate through it. If you're taking someone through a website or application with many steps, you want to show it in all its glory and in real time.

As a general rule, though, you should upload your visuals because:

- By uploading your content, you can smoothly navigate through all the content in your meeting. This is the biggest reason to upload your content rather than simply share screens. Have you ever done a presentation and stopped speaking to your PowerPoint slides to go to a flip chart to make a point, then led a discussion, and then gone back to your presentation? Of course you have, and by uploading your content you can easily duplicate that experience. Most platforms also let you rename your content so you can tell the difference between "whiteboard 1" and "whiteboard 4" when in a hurry.

- You have access to your entire meeting dashboard. When what you're presenting takes place in a defined area of the screen, you can readily manage the rest of the meeting at the same time. Watch the participants list for who's coming and going. Check the chat for relevant questions and comments. Easily annotate the screen to highlight important information and make it more memorable.

- You can easily pass "presenter" power no matter what you're showing at the moment or whose information it is. When sharing your screen, the visual you're showing pretty much needs to be on your computer. What's terrific about uploading the presentation is that, at the click of a mouse, anyone can take over. This is terrific when you have co-presenters in your meeting or when you need some help. Your co-pilot can take over at any time and you can enlist any meeting participant very easily.

Here's how you upload content in WebEx. Your PowerPoint files, video clips, pictures and documents will be under "File (Including Video):

Cisco WebEx Event Center - Leading Effective Virtual Meetings

| File | Edit | Share | View | Communicate | Participant | Event | Help |

Quick S | My Desktop   Ctrl+Alt+D   Whiteboard

File (Including Video)...

Application   ►

Whiteboard   Ctrl+Alt+N

Web Content...

Web Browser...

Multimedia...

My Event Window

BEST PRACTICE: The best thing you can do for your meeting's success is to prepare as much content as possible in advance. By having your whiteboards, presentations and other content ready before the meeting, you have less to distract you from being in the moment and maintaining your focus. Then you can avoid uncomfortable delays by switching seamlessly from one piece of content to another.

Here's where you manage your content in Lync 2013. Notice that it's a different model, but you will then see everything you've uploaded in Shared Content.

When you upload PowerPoint files and other documents, you have some extra capabilities.

Of course you can easily navigate through the slides using the "forward" and "back" arrows, but you also get some additional superpowers.

- You can jump ahead and back by using thumbnails or a dropdown menu. We've all planned presentations that had to be curtailed because of time or because the content isn't relevant. Maybe during Q and A someone asks you to share another piece of content again. Rather than scroll through the slides, you can just confidently go to the visual you want to share. Additionally, by seeing the thumbnails (hidden from your audience) it's simpler to transition from one visual to the next. It also doesn't hurt that you will actually know what's coming next.

- Most platforms let you read the Notes page in PowerPoint on screen during your presentation. Unless, of course, you have 50+ year old eyes and a small screen. Then just go old school and print them out like I do.

- Annotation and highlighting can make up for limited PowerPoint skills. Color, light and motion help people remember information better. Circle key words, underline stress points, or point out specific data on your most complicated charts. Let's face it, building animation into your presentation can be arduous and time-consuming, it's so much easier to just grab a highlighter or circle what you want your viewers to remember.

Polling, Surveys and Interaction Tools

Remember that what we're trying to do is get our work done. We need to gather useful information, build relationships that extend beyond this single meeting and get our darned work done. The interaction in your meeting should be purposeful and productive.

Most webmeeting platforms allow you to interact in several ways, both formal and informal.

Why You Want To Use These Tools

In meetings, constant feedback is critical. Sometimes you have serious votes, sometimes a quick show of hands, and sometimes you just look in their eyes for glimmers of consciousness, hoping they don't look like extras from The Walking Dead. Online, the looking-in-their-eyes part is nearly impossible, but there are still plenty of ways to engage them and get useful feedback.

The ability to incorporate these tools also serves a deeper function than simply knowing what people are thinking. By having to click on an icon or vote, you are engaging people physically—they are not simply passive observers. The more they actually *do* something in a meeting, the more likely they are to stay involved.

Also, people being human and all, color, action and humor are all part of keeping them interested and engaged. These features are what takes a good virtual meeting beyond the capability of a traditional conference call (and makes it pretty much worth the extra effort).

Let's start with the simplest tools and move up the (technical) food chain.

The "Raise Hand" Button

I remember speaking to a client who was bemoaning the lack of feedback and interaction when doing virtual sales calls. "Well, what would you do if you were in the room with those people?" I asked.

"Just ask for a show of hands," he replied.

"You know there's a button there that says, 'raise hand', right?" A sudden chagrined hush came over the conversation. When we talk about how most people don't use the tools at their disposal, this is exactly what I'm talking about.

If there's a little icon that looks like a raised hand, I'm betting that will create an icon next to your name that looks like a raised hand. This is great for when you want to ask a question or contribute to the conversation. Remember that, as a presenter, you need to scan periodically to see if anyone has their hand up.

I like to have everyone use the button at the beginning of the meeting just to make sure they know where it is, and how to use it.

Also remember to have people lower their hand once they've asked their question so you don't get confused. This is also good for quick, informal voting without going to the trouble of creating formal pools using the survey tools.

 BEST PRACTICE: This might seem unnecessary, but it actually happened to me. When encouraging people to "raise their hands", remind them it's a button on the screen and they shouldn't actually sit there in their office with their hand up. The only reason I noticed is I saw the participant on webcam looking frustrated because I wasn't calling on him.

It's happened, and it's embarrassing for all concerned.

Other Icons and Emoticons

Many platforms like WebEx (pictured above), Adobe Connect and more offer multiple quick feedback tools. You can give applause, offer a thumbs up or thumbs down (which are great for quick votes and getting input) or tell the presenter to speed up, slow down, or you're stepping out of the meeting for a moment.

BEST PRACTICE BEST PRACTICE: Set the tone for the meeting with your own choice of icons. If it's an informal meeting, don't be afraid to be a little silly by using the different pictures and encouraging others to use them as well (I like to use the "party hat" icon when someone shows up late as a way of teasing them without mortifying them). Applause, embarrassed smileys, and other icons can actually create a relaxed mood that encourages honest interaction.

If it's a more formal meeting, direct them to use certain icons like check marks, or "thumbs up" or "thumbs down". Usually people will use what you encourage them to use.

Here are just some of the feedback tools you can use informally in WebEx:

If you use Microsoft Lync, you'll notice they don't have these specific tools, but in the emoticon list there are plenty of ways to offer feedback (laughing smileys, sad smileys, Xs and checkmarks can serve the same purpose, they just appear in the chat window . Why Microsoft feels the need to give you all kinds of silly icons and only a few practical ones (then bury the practical ones at the bottom of the list) is a mystery but it's, you know, Microsoft.

Microsoft smilies and emoticons:

Use Annotation Stamps for Quick Voting.

How often have you gotten a suggested list of actions, or created a brainstorm, then needed to separate the great ideas from the silly suggestions? Rather than do a roll-call vote, just let them use their own annotation tools like stamps (stars, check marks, X's or arrows) to make their choice.

Remember, people stay engaged when they're actually *doing* something.

In another chapter we'll take a look at different ways to vote, and formats for meetings, but for now we're talking down and dirty feedback when you need it.

Polling and Surveys

One of the really cool features of webmeetings is the ability to conduct colorful, interactive formal polls of the audience to do audience analysis. What do they know about the topic? How do they feel about it? Have they actually learned anything?

This tool can be very useful. It gathers information, yes. You can often prepare polls and surveys in advance to make running the meeting easier. It also does the math, tells you who gave you what answer and saves it for posterity, all while using lots of colors and flashing lights to wake people up.

Among some of the things you can do with these tools are:

- Decide whether you want to see individual results or not. Maybe you're asking how many people feel confident using a software tool, and you want to see who is comfortable and who might not be ready to solo. Not everyone is comfortable admitting their ignorance, so you can set the poll to show you, as the host, who gives you what answer.

- Save the results. Many tools allow you to save the poll results. Did the team vote to focus on the Johnson account before doing anything else? You might need evidence to take back to your boss. You might also have to remind people that when stuff hits the fan, they did vote to take that particular course of action. This is also extremely helpful when you're doing training and need to test whether people actually learned anything.

- Create the polls in advance (and sometimes reuse them). There's a lot of clicking around when creating these polls. If you try to do this while leading the meeting, listening to the discussion and stressing about what's onscreen, you'll hurt yourself. Many platforms allow you to create your polls well in advance of the event. Take advantage of that. If you're doing a series of large meetings or the same training to numerous groups, have the polls prepared and save them on your computer in the same file you keep your PowerPoint visuals, handouts and other material associated with that topic. It shortens the setup time.

- Inject (appropriate) humor into your meetings. Just because the work you're doing is serious, doesn't mean you can't occasionally lighten the mood. I like to throw humor into the polls just to break the tension on occasion. (Very often in my meetings the survey answers are "Yes", "Not really"and "I'd rather poke my eyes out with a stick". The answers can be very telling). Remember, though, humor should be appropriate to the situation and the level of the corporate food chain attending your event.

BEST PRACTICE: The default setting for most of these survey tools is to hide the results until voting is finished. I usually change that setting so that people can see the numbers climb. This not only is colorful and wakes participants up, but seeing others vote (along with how many people haven't voted yet) encourages the laggards to keep up with the other kids. Nobody wants to be the guy who wasn't paying attention. Maybe someone isn't comfortable admitting they need more training until they see everyone else feels as ignorant as they do. This is a good thing.

Chat and the Q and A Function

One of the most important functions of a meeting is talking to each other. We give serious input. We make silly jokes. We introduce ourselves and get to know one another. Yet when we meet online, there is often a tendency to limit this input.

Sometimes this is for technical reasons. It's hard to talk when you can't see each other. We worry about talking over one another, and many online programs are Voice Over Internet Protocol (VOIP) which means when more than one person speaks at a time the sound cuts out and can be very frustrating. Fortunately webmeetings give us an additional way to communicate...the chat function.

Many people (dare I suggest the majority are older?) find chat either distracting or impersonal. Many new presenters are afraid it will become a distraction and try to limit the chat that takes place. They worry that people will say something inappropriate or off topic. The only response to that is to ask if those things every happen in a live meeting? How do you handle those situations? The same facilitation and leadership skills apply to managing the chat.

In fact, to a couple of generations of workers, writing in a little box and sending your thoughts into the ether is a perfectly natural way to "talk" to each other. Facebook, Twitter, chat, instant messaging and twitter are a natural part of communication.

Use These Tools When...

Think of the conference calls you've been on. We often have the same challenges we do during web meetings. We hear from the same people all the time. Some folks dominate the conversation, some need to be noodged to speak up. Some just disappear from the meeting entirely. It's no different with webmeetings, except that you have an additional way for people to put their two cents in.

Using chat can give your introverts a chance to participate, get questions lined up and create a permanent record of everyone's opinion on important topics. It serves both a synchronous (everyone talking at the same time to each other) and asynchronous (you can go back over time and refer to it) function.

Most chat functions allow you to keep a permanent record of what is said. This isn't (or at least shouldn't be) a way to keep tabs on who makes inappropriate statements or who takes part and who doesn't. It is, however, a great way to have a reference document of questions asked, what people actually thought about a topic, or track action items.

There's also another tool, kind of a subset of the chat dedicated specifically to Questions and Answers. This is a terrific tool (as we'll see in a minute) for easily separating questions from other chat. It also allows both written answers for all to see in perpetuity and get private, personal answers to questions without derailing the entire meeting.

When to Use the Q and A Function

- You have a large or particularly active group. The best use of having a separate Q and A function is to help manage the flow of information and pick the questions out of the other relevant comments and pithy commentary that naturally arises during your meetings. (Ahem). Seriously, if you expect a large number of questions this is an easy way to get them in queue.

- You can answer both publicly and privately. Not everyone is comfortable sharing their questions in an open forum. Sometimes it's because they are of a confidential or personal nature. Sometimes people have a specific question that isn't worth derailing the entire meeting for, and sometimes…well, while we constantly say there are no stupid questions…there are some that sure appear that way.

- You have a co-pilot. For all the reasons we've mentioned, it's sometimes a good idea to separate questions from the general conversation. Of course, that's one more thing you need to manage. If you have a co-pilot or someone you can designate to manage the chat for you it's one less distraction to take away from your focus. Additionally, if you have someone answering questions as they come in, it actually encourages people to send more in. They know you're serious about encouraging the dialogue.

- You're doing the same meeting over and over. Many of us are responsible for large, "town hall" type meetings where we'll be presenting the same information to multiple groups. By keeping a log of questions, you can often prepare for the next meeting. Is there a common theme or set of concerns you need to address? Does it seem like they're not getting a certain point? Maybe you need to re-examine how you are presenting it

 BEST PRACTICE: Periodically go over the questions you get for consistency. Maybe you're not presenting the big picture as well as you should, or need to spend more time on specific audience-related examples. We can always get better at this.

The Chat Function

This is one of the features that elevates a well-run webmeeting above even a well-facilitated conference call. It adds additional input and visual interest to the meeting, but it requires conscious thought to use it well. Specifically:

- Encourage use of chat at the beginning of your meeting to get people kinesthetically engaged. Just telling people that chat isn't available doesn't mean they'll take advantage of it. Insist everyone send a chat message to the whole room. You can do it under the guise of "making sure it's working" or just to speed up the informal chatting that normally takes place in a traditional meeting but can feel like wasted time online.

- Just because it's familiar, don't assume everyone uses it correctly. Chat is more and more common in our lives, whether it's instant messaging or online tech support. Still, each platform is slightly different. It's very common to have frustrating problems derail your efforts to get everyone involved. If people are typing in the wrong box (like the chat room rather than the smaller box at the bottom…and don't look at me like that, it happens more than you'd think) or they send what they thought was a private message to the entire meeting, it can put a crimp in the flow of conversation.

- Your introverts will love it. Not everyone is comfortable speaking in front of a group or calling attention to themselves. Conversely, those who do speak up don't necessarily have the most value to add. Giving your introverts a more comfortable way to contribute isn't a bad thing.

- So will those with less-than-ideal English skills. In our global workplace, we are often working with people from different countries and cultures. A common complaint is that many of these folks don't speak up in meetings and on calls. But if someone is unsure of how to say something, or they are constantly being asked to repeat themselves because the group can't understand them or decipher their accent, they will be reluctant to participate. Many people find their written English is clearer than their spoken English. Give them a chance to participate.

- We reveal a lot about ourselves…and that's a good thing. The things we laugh at, the comments we make, the small contributions to conversations are often how we learn about each other and form working relationships. Encourage an appropriate level of humor, informality and candor with your team. Unless you're meeting with the CEO or a client company, who cares if someone puts up a little smiley with a party hat on? If you need to step in and coach individuals, that's okay. People abuse this feature far less than you'll think.

BEST PRACTICE: One way to encourage participation from people you haven't heard from or you suspect have more to contribute is to use private chat to send them a gentle nudge. This is much kinder than simply calling on them and potentially embarassing them, which will certainly put a chill on any further participation.

Webcams and Video

Maybe the most enticing promise of virtual meetings is also the one that lags the furthest behind the reality. The use of webcams and streaming video is really tempting, and the platform providers will tell you in glowing terms how easy it is to use. The reality is that meeting leaders need to be strategic and slightly pessimistic in its use...at least for now.

As we get more used to watching streaming videos online, we want to share that experience. Is everyone watching the same clip of your latest product or are they watching cat videos on YouTube? Many tools now allow you to push video to your audience for a shared viewing experience.

However, successful use of videos in your meeting depends on available bandwidth, computing speed, what equipment you're using to participate in the meeting and the number of folks getting together. While we're all about using all the available technology, using it wisely still takes thought and planning.

Why you want to use these tools

The main attraction of video, of course, is that it accomplishes the main goal of meetings. We get to see and hear who we're working with. We can put faces to names, and get all kinds of visual cues about our teammates' competence and credibility.

Remember that you want to add value to your meeting without frustrating your audience or bringing things to a screeching halt. Does the value any tool brings outweigh the problems it might create?

Streaming Video

Showing video clips can be really helpful if you:

- Keep it short. Streaming video eats up a ton of bandwidth and computing power. One idea to reduce the stress is to keep video clips short (under 3 minutes) to reduce the amount of buffering it will take, and how much computer horsepower it will require. Some platforms limit the size of video clips to 5 MB, so be sure to test any video you plan to show. Rather than show a long clip, which can actually make people tune out (ever fallen asleep in front of the TV?) break the video into smaller, logical chunks and discuss after each piece.

- Upload your video as a file. Many platforms like WebEx and Adobe Connect allow you to upload your video just like you'd upload documents. This means that it will run smoother than if you're running it from your computer. This is also critical if you've uploaded your PowerPoint file and linked to the video, because those links won't work.

- Test the video stream outside of your network. There is nothing more embarrassing than planning an elaborate video presentation only to have it stutter, freeze or generally gum up the works. Before betting everything on the video, do everything you can to make sure it's going to work. Play it on the platform you're going to use for someone who isn't on your network, or is using different equipment like a tablet or smartphone.

 BEST PRACTICE: Plan for the worst, hope for the best. When in doubt, find a website where people can view the video on their own. YouTube is great for this (and works hand in glove with Google Hangouts).

Webcams

What you want is to maximize the power of seeing each other while minimizing potential distractions and problems. Webcams work much better than streaming video, but they still have their technical challenges.

 BEST PRACTICE: If you find your webcam image is not synching audio to video (do you look like a badly dubbed foreign movie? Unless you're warning them of Godzilla's impending arrival it can look really odd) try changing the setting. High Definition sounds lovely, but it's often unnecessary for day to day interaction, especially if you all know each other. Lower the quality of the image and, ironically, you'll improve the quality of the interaction.

There's one thing you must always do—test your webcam in advance of the meeting. Other than that obvious tip, webcams will add value most if you:

- Watch the lighting and environment. It's frustrating when the person you're speaking to can't actually make out your face because there's more light behind you than in front of you. You'll look like you're in the Witness Protection Program, and the video ceases to add any value. The easiest thing you can do is check for windows. If the light is coming in from behind you, close the curtains. Put a good lamp on your desk at 45 degrees behind your webcam to give you acceptable lighting without owning a TV studio.

- Don't sit too close or too far away. If you sit too far away, your face (which is the part of you people want to see) will be too indistinct to add value. If you're too close, it's a bit creepy. Most webcams use a "fisheye" type lens that distorts the visual outside of a certain distance. It's kind of like presenting through the peephole in an apartment door.

- Determine if everyone needs to see everyone else all the time. Because video sucks up bandwidth, the more cameras running at the same time the more problems you might cause. If you have a very small meeting of two-to-five people, it's not a big deal to have simultaneous video. If the meeting is bigger than that, consider changing the settings so that only the speaker or designated people are visible.

BEST PRACTICE: If you're not showing specific content, go to the full screen so everyone can see each other. Meeting kickoffs, introductions and Q and A sessions often don't have visuals to go with them, and they're the parts of the meeting where seeing each other matters most.

- Don't let the webcam become a distraction to the audience or the presenters. Most of the time, if we're showing a PowerPoint slide or sharing our screen, there's little value in having the audience see you on webcam as well. It's also distracting to worry about if they audience can see you in unguarded moments. Think about sharing the webcam where it adds the most value (like putting a face to a name during introductions) and then turning it off when you're presenting content that requires the audience to focus on the important information.

That's enough of an overview to get you started. If you haven't yet, go back to your web platform and poke around. Go ahead, we're not going anywhere.

Nothing we've discussed will help you if you don't experience it yourself in a safe environment. The time to try using a whiteboard is not when you've got your biggest client on the line, or when the boss is watching.

Here are some questions to ask yourself in preparation for the next session:

- What are the things you'd like to do in your meetings that haven't worked well?
- Based on what you've read, what tools would be most helpful in making that happen?
- How comfortable are you using those tools?
- What are you going to do about it?

With every meeting, it's important to consider what tools you will use to achieve your desired outcome and drive the work forward. If you know how to use them, you have no excuses. If you don't know how to use them, get on it.

We'll wait.

Breakout Rooms

Now's the time for the most important part of planning your webmeeting: creating an agenda that will help people show up prepared, enthusiastic, and accountable to everyone if they're not.

Some of the more robust webinar platforms have a feature that mimics what happens in many large, long meetings: you can break into small groups to work before coming together again. These "breakout rooms" are useful, but can be clunky to manage. If you're going to use them, make sure you manage the process very carefully.

Why you want to use these tools

Real brainstorming and great input usually comes from smaller, active groups. Your meeting may depend on such input. Breakout groups can help, just as they do in more traditional meetings.

Breakout rooms allow small groups of participants to meet privately, speak to each other, share documents, whiteboards and most of the other features of the main room. They can then save or share their work with the larger group.

A couple of things you want to bear in mind if using breakouts:

- You'll have to be very explicit about your directions. Unless people have used these tools before, there will be a lot of confusion and wasted time. Use short, step by step descriptions of what you want them to do and which tools to use.

- Appoint a team leader for each breakout group. Preferably this is someone comfortable with the technology who can patiently help the others catch up.

- Immediately upon sending people to the rooms, pop in to each room to ensure no one is lost in cyberspace, people understand the assignment and know how to begin.
- Manage time very carefully.
- Because of the technology involved (and it's all voodoo to me), carefully test your audio before deciding breakouts are critical to your success. Some systems only allow breakouts if you're all using the VOIP on their computers, others will only work with some phone conferencing systems.

BEST PRACTICE: If you're using breakout groups, it may be that your meetings are too long or too crowded. Maybe it's time to take a break, let people meet together and reconvene later.

If this is the only way to make things done, make sure you carefully document the assignment, timeframe and expectations so there's no wasted time or frustration, which can kill your meeting buzz.

Section 3:

Planning for Success - The Agenda

"Luck is a matter of preparation meeting opportunity."

Seneca the Younger

Creating a Really, Truly, Honest-to-Goodness, Powerful, Productive Agenda

Before you skip this chapter, and give me a smug, "I always send out an agenda", I want you to ask yourself: Do you send out an agenda, or do you send an invitation? They are not the same thing. Pretty much everyone sends a meeting invite. Precious few send out a powerful, productive agenda.

A really powerful and productive meeting requires people to participate, contribute and add value in a lot of little ways. This implies, of course, that they should actually show up prepared to participate, contribute and add value.

How's that going for you?

Ideally, before people ever log onto the webmeeting you want them to know what they must have, to show up on time, be prepared to participate, contribute everything you need from them and what's expected. As a manager, this allows you to have some confidence that you can start on time, get down to business, and hold people accountable if they don't perform as expected.

As an employee, you now know what the heck you're expected to do, and why meeting is more important than whatever it is you're doing (e.g., your "real work"). It also lets you know what your boss and teammates expect of you. Hopefully that matters enough to actually, you know, do it.

So just to be clear, the agenda might be included with the invitation, but they aren't the same thing.

What's the difference between an invitation and an agenda?

An invitation basically says, "Hey, there's a meeting at such-and-such a time, please block out the time". It might (if you've set the meeting up already) also include information such as the link to join the meeting, dial in information and the like. Here's what's in a typical meeting invitation:

- When the meeting starts (or is supposed to start).

- When it will end (more or less).

- You might even know the topic ("Status update on the Johnson project", or something equally non-committal).

- A link to join the meeting.

- A link to test whether the software will work on your network or computer—which will be roundly ignored until it's too late.

- A calendar function to automatically update your calendar.

- An email reminder notice some pre-determined time before the meeting.

Invitations are essentially placeholders. They contain the bare information to make sure people block time and show up. Ask yourself: would this be enough information to really prepare yourself for the meeting? Do people know what's expected of them? Certainly you can assume they will, being professionals and all. In fact, that assumption is largely unfair and doesn't help prepare people or hold them accountable in a fair, responsible way.

Here's what should be included in an effective agenda—and why. Bear in mind that it's always possible people will find a way to delete, misread, or altogether avoid your written instructions. If you've taken the time to put it out there, though, then it's on them, and you or their teammates can hold them accountable. You've done your part, and maybe they'll pay more attention next time.

Team culture and habits are defined, and maintained, over time. Have patience and stay consistent.

Meeting Logistics

This is the part most of us are pretty good at. If you want people to show up, prepared or not, they need to know when and how you'll meet. Whether you know this information when the meeting is first set up or not, it's a good idea to include it in the final agenda, just to be safe. Among the information you'll include:

- **Time of the meeting and when it will end.** Meetings that start and end on time are usually more productive and far less frustrating for both meeting leaders and participants. Explicitly suggest that they join 5-10 minutes before start time so you can all start on time. Put it in bold on the invitation, and include it in the reminders as well. If they join late, and use technology as an excuse, remind them that the invitation suggested they log on early. It is unlikely to happen twice.

- **How to test your connection in advance of the meeting.** One of the main reasons webmeetings start late is because people have challenges getting connected, or it takes longer than they expect because of plugins or unforeseen downloads. Many platforms automatically include a link that allows your invitees to test their equipment, bandwidth and software in advance of the meeting. Here's a crazy idea…encourage people to actually take advantage of it. Send a separate email if you really want to get their attention.

- **The meeting link with password information.** This is usually generated automatically if you invite attendees using the platform tools.

- **A tool to enter the meeting automatically into their calendar.** Even very smart, confident people seem to struggle with getting time zones right. Most of us have shown up for a conference call or meeting, only to discover it started a year earlier…or doesn't start for another hour. By using the calendar feature, they can automate the process of entering the event into their main calendar, which syncs with their phones and other tools. It also automatically does the math to convert whatever time you schedule to their time zone. Don't suggest they use it, make it a requirement.

- **Audio information.** Depending on your company's IT policies, this can get tricky. While some platforms allow you to use the platform itself for audio, some don't. Many offer telephone conferencing as well, or you have to use your company's audio.

- If they're using VOIP, try to have a headset with microphone. Yes, they can simply use the mic and speakers in their computer, but they (and everyone else) will be at the mercy of their surroundings. Sound quality is often uneven. Encourage (and if it's worth it, offer to spring for the cost of), an inexpensive USB headset with microphone.

- If they're dialing in, ensure that the phone information is on the same invitation or email as the log in information. Too often, especially if teams use the same conference bridge all the time, there's an assumption that everyone has that information already. What have we learned about assumptions?

- Landlines are better than cell phones. Seriously. Go old school. Old fashioned as it may seem, the simple fact is that landline telephones offer more stability and better sound quality than cell phones. Explicitly state they should use their land lines if at all possible. Again, a headset is a good idea. Cell phones on speaker are a court of last resort.

- Who's invited and why. If it's the usual team members, and you've all been meeting for a while, that's great. When teams are forming, though, or you are going to have unexpected attendees, your team should know not just who's there, but their roles(s)

BEST PRACTICE: As odd as it seems, the best way to ensure meetings start on time is to avoid meetings that start at the top of the hour. Why? Because if your meeting starts at 2, odds are they're on another call or meeting that is scheduled to end at 2. The laws of physics being what they are, they can't actually be in two meetings at the same time. Even if the other meeting ends on time, people need recovery time to plan, log on, and attend to biological needs before sitting down to another meeting. Try scheduling for 15 or 30 minutes after the hour. You'll be surprised how many people actually attend.

The Purpose of the Meeting

Have you ever shown up for a meeting not knowing what's going to be covered, or why you're needed? If your attendees are showing up asking themselves why they're there…well you're already off to a very iffy start.

The simplest way to ensure people come prepared to help the meeting be successful, is for them to know what the purpose of the meeting is. This should be explicit and specific. Basically, what you want to do is complete this sentence, then cut and paste it into the agenda:

Purpose: The purpose of the meeting is to _____

"Status Update" doesn't tell anyone what the exact purpose of the meeting is or what will happen. This purpose presents a clear expected outcome: "The purpose of this meeting is to reach consensus on next steps for the Johnson account. Each division should be prepared to present their current milestones and define what assistance they will require. We will require everyone's best thinking and input on this project." is much more specific.

The reason for this specificity should be obvious. "Status" is fairly vague, and you may not get the exact information you require without some wasted time and extra effort. If people clearly understand what the meeting is supposed to achieve, they have a very clear idea of why they're there and what's expected of them.

This has a long-term impact on future meetings as well. If your meetings are perceived as having a clear purpose, and that purpose is consistently supported and achieved, there will be a more positive approach to your meetings, especially if it's followed by…

Defined, clear, specific, desired outcomes as well as a timeline.

If the purpose of the meeting is the big picture reason for meeting, the desired outcomes are what need to be accomplished during the time together. They are the tangible outcomes that determine whether you have been successful or not.

The easiest way to know if a meeting has been successful is to know that you accomplished what you set out to do. Talking about a problem, or brainstorming solutions, is not an outcome. Those are activities that take place during your time together. The desired outcome is a solution everyone can agree on.

Try to be as specific as you can so there's no question that you achieved your goals. Know what you want to achieve, and make it plain to the audience as well.

Share your expectations with the audience.

Agenda Items and Timeline: Here's what we'll do in our time together _____

Meeting Outcomes: At the end of our meeting, we will have _____

Is anyone going to be unclear on what will happen or how the success of the meeting will be measured?

What activities or functions will take place during the meeting?

What will actually happen during the meeting to achieve those outcomes and what does that mean to your attendees? "Brainstorming" is helpful. But "We expect to hear each of your opinions on potential pitfalls and challenges with the Johnson account" is very specific. And, of course, it's easy to measure. Someone either contributed or they didn't. You heard from Willie or you didn't.

Simply put, you want to tell the audience, "This is what we'll be doing during the meeting, be prepared". You're both playing fair with your attendees, and able to hold them clearly accountable for their preparation and participation.

Again, a simple line in the agenda can serve the purpose:

During our time together we'll _____ and _____ so that we're ready for the client meeting on Thursday.

Notice that we've also made it clear how delivering these outcomes impacts the "real" work of the team, which is to service the Johnson account. (This account seems to be a lot of trouble, it better be profitable. Just saying…)

What specifically is expected of the attendees, and how do they prepare?

Again, if you're going to have people excited about attending, prepared to actively participate, and engaged throughout, you have to let them know exactly what's expected of them. Are there specific speakers? What are their roles? What does "be ready" even mean?

One of the most common frustrations is sending documents out in advance only to realize as the meeting is started that they aren't ready to have the discussion.

"Here's the document we'll discuss during our meeting, be prepared to share your thoughts" sounds pretty clear, but is it?

Were you specific about the fact they were to "read" (which could mean study in depth, scan, or even just be vaguely aware of its existence) and be "prepared to discuss" (which to many people means the usual people will be heard from and the rest of us ignored), and "your thoughts" (whatever that means)?

"We urge you to carefully read the following document(s) and expect to hear from each of you what this means to your job and your role in this project", is a very different kind of expectation. Can anyone reading that message not understand that you expect them to actually speak about what they've read? Merely lurking is not an option.

The more specific you are about your expectations, the easier it is for people to meet (and often surpass) them. When you're describing the preparations and activities be as precise and unequivocal as you can.

"Brainstorm" or "suggest alternatives" is much plainer and more precise than "share your thoughts".

A simple, clear description of what you expect everyone to do in advance of, and during, the meeting is best:

To make the most of our time together please:

1. State what they need to read or prepare to contribute.

2. Describe what activities will happen during the meeting and how they will participate.

Now, about those documents, prework and attachments.

In order to be ready to work in a meeting, people often need to read, think about, and prepare their contributions. How do we ensure that people know which documents and reference materials they need to access in order to be properly prepared? Most of us send them as attachments to the invitation or in separate emails.

That's the problem.

Certainly, the onus is on meeting participants to prepare and keep track of communication. That's very little comfort, though, as the meeting time ticks closer and we're answering panicky emails asking for us to please resend whichever version of whichever document they need.

The problem with email attachments is they're a terribly inefficient way to send valuable information that people need to save and refer to. Why? Because people don't give email the respect it deserves.

We delete email without reading it. Or we drag and drop it into sub folders then forget where we put it. Or the file is too big to transfer effectively.

We should be leveraging all the technology available to us, especially tools like shared files, SharePoint and databases. This technology is the fastest way to access information when you need it, control access and security, and makes version control simple. It also downloads the documents directly to useful places on our computers or devices so we can access them almost anywhere.

And of course, when in doubt, we can access the meeting technology itself (see the section on Attachments and File Transfer) so people can download the information without disrupting the meeting or wandering off to their email.

 BEST PRACTICE: Rather than scramble to send and re-send documents, only to have people worry about which version they're getting, stop enabling the craziness. When they ask you to email the document, send a response with the link to where they can find the document themselves in their shared files or databases. Not only does it take the same amount of time, but you begin to reinforce the idea that people know perfectly well where to find information, and they're responsible for getting the information on their own.

Remember, you're not just trying to get through this particular meeting (in which case you would just send the file and mutter about them under your breath). You're laying the groundwork for future meetings and creating a competent, self-directed, empowered team that can get work done without constantly dragging you into it.

The more people leverage technology to access information on their own, the more it frees you from the grunt work and allows you to hold them, and each other, accountable.

The biggest change for many of us is to model using these tools ourselves, and resisting the short-term solution by just sending the email and calling them names under our breath.

The simplest way to build this into your agenda is to simply fill in the blank:

In order to make the best use of everyone's time, please download the following document(s) and be prepared to _____.

So, a clear, specific agenda goes a long way to ensure a meeting's success. For the meeting participants, it's immensely helpful. The agenda sets context, which answers the pressing questions of "Why bother?" and "What's in this for me?" It helps people be truly prepared and set expectations. It also gives them the criteria for success.

For meeting leaders, it eliminates a lot of the busy-work and stress that often goes into leading painless and productive meetings. It also helps you work with the team in the future because you've created clear, explicit performance metrics that increase the likelihood of success. For those of us who manage people, it allows you to hold people accountable and coach them going forward.

Save time and be more consistent

If we are honest with ourselves, we'd admit that a good agenda is always a good idea. We also know we don't create them nearly often enough, relying on automated meeting invitations and emails. The process of creating an agenda every time and making it consistently part of your meetings is easier than you'd think.

First, most platforms allow you to create templates for email invitations and meeting reminders. If that's the case, create an invitation that allows you to create simple agendas. If you don't have that ability, create a simple document template (in Word or something similar) that you can simply cut and paste vital information into.

Here's a simple template that you can just "plug and play" for every occasion:

Simple Meeting Agenda Template

Meeting Logistics

- Time of the meeting and when it will end
- How to test your connection in advance of the meeting
- The meeting link with password information
- A tool to enter it automatically in their calendar
- Audio information

Purpose: The purpose of the meeting is to _____

Agenda Items and Timeline: Here's what we'll do in our time together _____

Meeting Outcomes: At the end of our meeting, we will have_____

During our time together we'll _____ and _____ so that (tell them how this will impact their work or project)

To make the most of our time together please:

1. State what they need to read or prepare to contribute
2. Describe what activities will happen during the meeting and how they will participate

In order to make the best use of everyone's time and reduce confusion, please download the following document(s) (include link to any documents or pre-work) and be prepared to_____(Use behavior specific words)_____

How Big Should Your Meeting Be?

One of the most common questions we get in our training programs is; how many people can we have on our meetings? This, of course, is the wrong question. The real question is, how many *should* you have?

Remember that with any meeting we've been discussing form follows function. You should have the right number of people to accomplish your prescribed outcome.

The simple way to think about it is this: the larger the group, the less interaction you'll solicit. This happens in traditional meetings as well.

Small groups tend to be less formal, and conversation flows naturally. The more people you add to the gathering, the more reticent people are to interrupt, ask questions or even participate at all. Additionally, large meetings tend to be one-way, "hold your questions til the end" affairs.

That's fine if you are doing "town hall" type meetings like you'd do to make a major announcement. If you want to do some deep down brainstorming and problem solving, you want a smaller, more focused team with only the right people involved.

As a rule of thumb, the proper number of people for a meeting depends on your desired outcomes:

- Companywide announcements with limited Q &A can hold 100 plus people.
- Announcements or other updates where questions are going to be common should hold <50 people.
- Announcements that impact a specific region or group should include the people in that group.
- Training shouldn't have one person more than you'd have in a traditional classroom event. At

GreatWebMeetings.com that means we cap our classes at 10 people so everyone gets a chance to participate and get instructor attention.

- Problem solving teams shouldn't have more than 10 people unless you have breakout rooms or a really experienced team.

- Remember, the number of people your platform allows is a maximum, not a recommendation.

Section 4:

Just Before, During and After the Meeting

"If you had to identify, in one word, why the human race has not achieved, and never will achieve its full potential, that word would be 'meetings'".

Dave Barry

Getting the Meeting Started

If I asked you to imagine how too many virtual meetings get started, it would look a little like this:

The participants trickle in anywhere from five minutes early to heaven-knows-when. There are some hellos exchanged among the "Can you hear me's?" and the "Is this thing ons?" A flurry of activity happens as the leader attempts to say hello to everyone while loading her own presentation.

Finally, usually up to ten minutes after the scheduled start time, the leader gets some semblance of order and jumps right into the content "so as not to waste everyone's time" (If thoughts were audible, a shout of "Too late!" would echo through the land). There are some stilted, very perfunctory introductions, and then finally, mercifully, you get down to work.

If this sounds familiar, then like most thinking mortals you're aware that your meeting is already off to a very bad start. As the leader, you're frazzled and stressed before you even get started and you've wasted precious time. Your participants are equally stressed, and feeling like they're time's wasted. Their worst suspicions about how this is all going to go…well they're being confirmed in glorious Technicolor.

It doesn't have to be this way. Yes, there will always be people coming in late, and some chaos is to be expected. After all, traditional meetings aren't run or attended by automatons, either. People's behavior is messy and chaotic. But every webmeeting doesn't need to be a car wreck either.

One of my favorite quotes is "Well begun is half done". This has been attributed to both Aristotle and Mary Poppins. (Seriously, Google shows it both ways.) Claim Aristotle said it, and everyone will be impressed and think you've read Aristotle. Regardless of who said it first, it is undoubtedly true.

The first steps to ensuring the meeting's success actually happen before the meeting officially begins.

Before the meeting starts

Not to nag or be redundant, but the most important thing you can do before a meeting is get a proper agenda out to the audience well in advance of the meeting. At least 24 hours is about right…it's not so long that people will forget about it, yet gives people plenty of time to actually prepare based on the information you give them. (Take a look at the chapter on Creating a Truly Honest-to-Goodness Powerful and Productive Agenda).

BEST PRACTICE: If your platform allows it, load items for the meeting as you think of them so there's less to do in the few minutes before the event. Seriously; the more you do in advance, the less you have to think about just before your important meeting.

Another thing you should do well in advance is give anyone who is a planned presenter access to the meeting (if you're unclear on this, see the section on Permissions) so they can upload any content in plenty of time to be relaxed and prepared. PowerPoint files, documents that will be shared and whiteboards can all be locked and loaded.

At the very least, try and log onto the meeting a half hour before the scheduled start time. This will allow you and other participants to connections, load relevant material and reduce the craziness of multiple people logging in all at once.

A couple of points here:

- I'm not crazy. Remember we are only suggesting you log on and open the meeting. You can still answer email, talk on the phone or do whatever you have to do to prepare.

- Don't worry about missing something. Most platforms have either an audio (like a little "ding" noise, or a video (flashing icon on your task bar) that will alert you as people enter or send you chat messages.

 BEST PRACTICE: Create a whiteboard with the dial-in information and any logistics and set that as the first thing participants see when they log on. This will prevent repeated calls for the dial-in information (which you've sent at least twice, but don't dwell on it or you'll make yourself crazy).

As people start to "arrive", chat them in

When you're holding a traditional meeting, what usually happens? People filter into the room, and as they do, you greet them. The conversation is usually informal, casual and designed to strike a cordial relationship. "How was your weekend?" "Did you see the game last night?" "Doughnuts are over there, but the coffee stinks"…all the usual stuff co-workers say to each other to create a collegial environment.

Maybe you need help with the handouts, or want to ask someone to make sure they share something with the group they told you earlier. All of these things can help the overall meeting.

The same things can happen in an online meeting, if you're already there and prepared. I like to greet people both by voice and chat. This is especially helpful when the audio is on the phone and requires a second connection.

There are several ways to use chat as people enter

Just as you greet people when they come in, you can do the same using the chat feature. I like to send a private chat message to each person as they enter the virtual meeting room. This serves both a social function and a more practical one with long-term effects.

A private chat message helps build social connections. You can ask about someone's weekend. Ask how the surgery went, the kids are, or how much they lost on the Bears without exposing that conversation to the whole group. It's also a great chance to ask for assistance with the meeting.

Maybe they have something you'd like them to share with the group, and you can ask them to prepare their comments. Perhaps you need an assistant to help scribe on the whiteboard. Just as you'd speak to people as they enter a "real" meeting room, you can do the same via keyboard and voice.

This is also a really good opportunity to check that they're prepared for the meeting. Nothing wrong with asking "have you read that document…" If the answer is no, tell them there's still time. If the answer is "Can you resend it?" Send the link in chat and gently coach them to be ready next time.

As you can probably figure, there's something more practical at work here than simply making nice with each other.

When many people log into a virtual meeting, there's an expectation that they can just put the phone on mute and go do something else. When they have to respond to a personal message, they are forced to give you their attention. Additionally, the act of typing a response engages them kinesthetically…once they have participated, they are more likely to pay attention and stay engaged. Do this even if you've checked in with them verbally.

BEST PRACTICE: Once you've started the meeting, it's still important to greet latecomers. Designate someone to greet them and fill them in on what's happening ("Hi Bill, glad you could make it—we're just going over the agenda") without interrupting the flow of the meeting. This is also a great way to handle questions about process or technical questions (especially re-sending the phone information). If you don't have a co-pilot, you can do it yourself by cutting and pasting a standard greeting.

If this is a one-time meeting, or it's a particularly large group, there's only so much you can do to limit the chaos. If this is a meeting with an intact team, coach participants who are late to send a chat message to everyone, rather than interrupt vocally, unless it's important. You (and everyone else) can see when they log on. The meeting doesn't have to screech to a halt whenever someone else joins.

Using the audio effectively

If the audio and webmeeting are connected, you may hear a signal when the audio is connected, and people will be able to see the meeting and speak or hear at the same time. If the meeting hasn't started yet, say hi quickly and confirm they are hearing everything fine.

Leave the phone lines open until the meeting starts. If people want to say hello to each other, make jokes or just vent…isn't that what they'd do in a normal, face-to-face meeting?

Once the meeting starts, take control of the audio:

- Turn off the "join meeting" announcement (the dings, gongs and other noises that announce someone has joined).

- Unless the meeting has many attendees (more than 12- 15) don't mute everyone's phones. Act like you trust them to do it themselves, and most people will behave like adults (more on this in the section on Ground rules). This will make them aware that they're muted, and will have to physically unmute to speak up.

- Don't keep stopping every time someone joins the meeting unless they have a specific, important role like guest speaker or senior management. A quick chat message will suffice to greet them.

- Encourage head sets and microphones, rather than using the mics and speakers built into their devices.

- Know where the "mute all" button is if it's necessary.

 BEST PRACTICE: Do a formal roll-call once and do it right. Once the meeting has started, use the participant list in the webmeeting to check if people are present and paying attention. This helps those who've already said hello to stay engaged, lets everyone else know who's there, and lets those who join late or all at once still get recognized.

Kick off the meeting and get everyone focused

Now is the moment to truly kick off your event. There are several things you want to accomplish in the next few minutes:

- Begin the meeting as close to the announced start time as you can.

- Focus everyone's attention on the task at hand.

- Control the environment as best you can.

- Set ground rules for how the meeting will be run.

- Share a clear, effective, agenda and timeline.

- Introduce anyone that needs introducing.

- Set a professional tone so people will actually believe this will be a productive session.

- Establish your credibility as a leader.

- Give yourself a fighting chance to succeed.

Begin the meeting as close to the announced start time as you can

Try to start as close to the announced start time as you can. When you have over half of your attendees, or at least have the critical participants, get started. Those who are late will catch up. Maybe they might be inspired to get there earlier for the next one. That's how cultures are built.

Focus everyone's attention

When you're ready to start the meeting, announce the fact clearly, "Okay everyone, let's get started. We have a lot to do, and we want to make the best use of everyone's time." Notice that you're not starting on time for your benefit, but for everyone's benefit—to make good use of their time. You've basically told the meeting that it's about them. Not a bad message to send to your team.

 **BEST PRACTICE:** One good way to get everyone to pay attention in a hurry is to use the "raise hand" button (which not only gets them to listen but engages them with the software). Ask the audience, "If you can hear me and you're ready to go, push the raise hand button". This is also a good tool to focus people when returning from breaks.

Control the environment as best you can

In a face-to-face meeting room you can control a lot. You can close curtains, call for order, set rules about when people can use their phones, and adjust the temperature in the room (for all the good that will do you. Someone will be either too hot or too cold. (Usually, both at the same time). Online, you have less direct control over everyone's working environment.

This is one of the biggest concerns for those of us who run virtual meetings. We have the awful suspicion they're answering email or playing Minesweeper instead of actually paying attention. If we're not careful, it can become a self-fulfilling prophecy.

Many platforms have some form of "attention indicator", which is nothing more sophisticated than an icon on the presenter's dashboard (usually an exclamation mark or a warning triangle, but it varies) that shows when someone's looking at a screen other than the meeting platform .

This is not designed for you to immediately nag people to pay attention, but it should give you an indication of how much attention people are paying to what's going on. If someone looks elsewhere for a moment, it's not a big deal. If half your audience seems to be elsewhere, you might want to do something about that. You could generate some discussion. Or take a bio break and reconvene in five minutes when people are, umm, refreshed.

One good recommendation is to share the "attention meter's" existence with the audience. If they know that YOU know they're not paying attention, they're more likely to make the effort.

When we talk about the virtual meeting environment, we're talking about:

- Audio. What are your expectations around leaving phone lines muted or live? Does your system have "on hold "music that will kick in if they put the conference on mute? If they are going to mute their lines, remind people that if they want to speak, they'll have to unmute themselves. You'd be surprised how often people start speaking, then realize no one can hear them.

- Email, Instant Messaging and multi-tasking. This is the big one for most of us, but it's easy to get overly paranoid. The first thing to remember is that not all multi-tasking is bad. People are often checking documents, looking up answers to questions on the group's behalf, and telling people they're in a meeting, they'll get back to them later. Set your expectations. If you want them to close other applications, say so. Let them know it's not because of your neediness, but because they're expected to participate.

BEST PRACTICE: One of the most successful tips to focus attention is one I learned from a client. People usually hear the "turn off email" announcement and shrug it off. Try using this line: "Please turn off email, instant message, and any applications on your computer that might suck up bandwidth. If you've ever been on a webmeeting that has crashed, it's usually because the

computer was using too much processing power, so the less y
computer is doing, the less chance of something bad happening.
Thanks".

Many people have an unhealthy fear of the technology, and will
be sufficiently concerned that they'll actually pay attention. After all,
you're asking for their benefit not your own need for attention. It's
also just true enough that your conscience will be clear.

Provide expectations to the audience

If you want your audience to hold questions until the end of your
time together (something I really, really don't recommend) they should
know that. Will you be calling on people throughout the meeting? If
you expect them to participate and ask questions as you go, they need
to know that as well. What are your expectations about using the chat
and other tools? It's important that you set a tone for your meetings
without sounding hectoring or nagging.

If they are new (or you suspect they're new) to the platform, you
will want to be very explicit about how to use the tools. Check out the
section on "Give them a tour".

Introduce yourself and each other

Virtual meetings are not just about transferring information, but
about getting to know and value the people you work with. An
important component of any meeting is creating an environment
where the people gathered actually get to know each other. How you
introduce yourself matters.

How do you want to introduce yourself to the audience?
Obviously, it depends on what they already know, but the first place to
start is visually: can they put a face (and voice and, hopefully,
personality) to the name?

Here are some tips to visually introduce yourself to the group.

- **If the group doesn't know you** use your webcam to say hello. Even if you don't use it throughout the meeting (see the section on Webcams and Video for more tips) you can at least say hello, and give the audience a sense of who you are and who they're dealing with.

- **If you don't have a webcam, or it's five in the morning, you haven't showered, and video is a decidedly bad idea…**you can still use visuals to help people get to know you. Post a picture of yourself along with some relevant biographical data on a PowerPoint slide or whiteboard.

- **Don't use the super-professional boring picture.** It's one thing to put a face to a name. You probably don't want to associate that face with the stiff, formal, corporate picture you're tempted to use. I always like to use less formal, candid (but not incriminating) photos. I have a couple that I have for just such occasions.

One is a head shot of me in a sports coat and smiling professionally…it's fine for most occasions. With my team, though, or when I'm trying to set a less formal environment I either use a more relaxed picture of me with my cockatiel Byron. It says, "I'm relaxed, I like birds and I'm a little weird." They're going to find out anyway, why not own it?

Let the others introduce themselves—be brief and relevant

If you work together all the time, it's not necessary to introduce yourself. If this meeting is with people you don't know this is a chance to connect. It's also their first impression of you. Are you just another corporate mouthpiece? Are you just a vendor with a hidden agenda?

Think about what your audience most wants to know. Relevant information can include three or four of these items of information. More than that, people tend to think you're either a blowhard or needy, or a needy blowhard. None of that works to your advantage):

- **Your name, position and role.** Position and role are not the same thing." VP of Corporate Services" doesn't tell anyone what you actually do every day. "I'm in charge of our company's internal processes and customer service" tells the customer what you actually do and sounds much weasel-y.

- **Relevant business experience.** Have you had experience with this customer or subject before? Why should your audience think you're bringing any value to the table? For example, if you're meeting with sales people, they want to know you've lived on commission or "carried a bag". In case you haven't noticed, sales people don't trust anyone who's never been in sales. That is also true of engineers, finance people and anyone with a very narrow focus. Do you have the foggiest idea what they do? Prove it.

- **Geography.** Where are you? Amazingly, this creates a lot of valuable team building as people discuss the weather, what your local team did over the weekend and who has a cousin nearby. Seriously, this is the kind of stuff that has people opening up and relaxing with each other.

- **Non-incriminating personal information.** If you're going to be working with people for a while, let them start to know you. Do you have kids? A driving passion? Many a good working relationship has begun over an argument about football teams.

- **Why you care about the topic at hand** Do you have personal experience with industrial accidents? Maybe that's why you're so excited about leading this safety training

Depending on the size of your audience, you might want to give everyone a chance to introduce themselves to the group. Keep these introductions focused and brief so you don't get off track (unless getting to know each other is the whole purpose of the meeting).

What will help is to put up a whiteboard or PowerPoint slide with guidelines. A simple example:

- Your name
- Where you are
- Your role
- One thing you want to get from this meeting or one question you really need answered

This lets them know that while you want to know about them, you need to keep on track. If you're new to the team, you will make some interesting judgments based on whether or not people can keep to the assignment. You'll find the ramblers, the know-it-alls and the extreme introverts very quickly.

If you have a large group, you obviously can't take the time to have everyone introduce themselves. If you have one minute to spare, though, there's a cool thing you can do to get people engaged and find out a little about them.

Use the public chat to ask a simple question. You'll get them physically interacting and engaged, and also will learn a bit about your audience. A good example is, "I want to make sure everyone's properly connected to the meeting, do me a favor please and type in the public chat where you are today, and what's the weather doing there?"

Of course, if the team meets together all the time, there's nothing wrong with a quick roll-call and on to business. Specifically…

Why are you meeting, and what are you trying to accomplish?

The most pressing questions in your participants' minds are: "Why am I here, and how is this more important than whatever else I could be doing?" The sooner you answer that, the more focused your audience will be. The longer you take to answer it, the more they'll fill in the blanks on their own. It's a sad fact of human nature that no one assumes the best case scenario.

The simplest and most effective way to do this is to refer to the agenda (you did send out a proper, honest-to-goodness agenda, right?). What are your purpose and outcome? Basically, you're answering their most important questions: here's what we need to do, and here's how we know we've done it.

This only takes two sentences, but might be the most important part of your opening. You've informed the audience why you need them and what the result of their work will be.

If you meet all the time, this tends to get pushed aside. attitude becomes "Hey it's the Tuesday Status Meeting…what do y think we're going to do?" We make a lot of assumptions about wh; everyone's thinking and doing, and it's amazing how often we're wrong. This is deadly to team engagement and morale.

One project team leader I know at a major New York bank takes this a step further. She starts every meeting by going back to the charter for the project. The message is unmistakable: the only reason to have this meeting is to move the project ahead. If it does that, we have time for it. If it doesn't directly impact the project, we don't have time. It keeps things very focused and the team is free to question the value of any activity or time spent that doesn't meet that criteria.

She's a very smart team leader, and very brave, because her team is free to call her on anything that seems off track or not valuable to the overall mission. It also works.

Set the tone for your meeting by making simple declarative sentences. "What we're here today to do is _____ and in the next hour we want to make sure we __ , _____ , ___". Congratulations, you've both set expectations and the metric that will determine how successful your meetings. Now all you have to do is meet those expectations.

Engage them right away

While I'm no rocket scientist, I do know one basic law of physics that applies to meetings of any kind; a body at rest stays at rest, a body in motion stays in motion. What does this have to do with kicking off your meeting?

If someone logs on, sits through introductions and doesn't actually do anything for a while they become very passive Then, when it's time for participation, they just can't be bothered to participate. Just as likely they have found something more exciting to do. Email is fascinating. So is trying to break your high score in Free Cell.

In a traditional meeting, people tend to stay focused (or at least pretend to) because they can be seen. Social propriety suggests you suck it up and play nicely. In cyberspace, no one can see you and you won't hurt anyone's feelings if you get distracted. Well, you will, but you won't have to see the look of pained disappointment on their face.

People need to be engaged physically, not just with their ears, but with their hands. If they're active and focused early on in the meeting, and consistently throughout, there is a better chance of them staying engaged.

You have tools like chat, raised hands, feedback and polling or surveys. While you don't want to create busy work, or waste too much time, this is a good way to kick things off and get their input. Here are a couple of tips:

- Kick off your meeting by asking for a "show of hands" (use the raise hand button or chat) to insist people let you know that they can hear you and are ready to start. That way they have to use the platform, and if they don't respond you can check on them. This will put them on notice, if nothing else. This is also good for when you take breaks and want to know everyone's back. I ask "If you are back and can hear me, raise your hand". When the hands are up, it's time to get back to work.

- Use polling and surveys constructively. Is there reading you've asked them to do? Use polling to determine how they felt about it. This will also send the message that you expect them to actually, you know, read stuff you send out. Polling is a great way to find out, not only objective information like knowledge, but how they're feeling about a certain topic. I find it a great way to inject humor into meetings without being too goofy. "How do you feel about the Bears getting their butts kicked last night?" is the kind of question we'd ask in a live meeting to break the ice and lighten the mood. It works online too...

Finally, there's a way to engage people that works, and yet seems to be counter-intuitive to most people:

Start with the most important action item on the agenda

We've all been on meetings that take so much time checking administrative tasks off, that by the time we get to the "good stuff" too much time has passed and we're frustrated, bored, or just past caring. If you want your people to be prepared, give great input, make good decisions and make them feel like their time is being honored, put first things first.

You'll get better ideas and energy from people while they're fresh and focused on the task at hand. There will also be a better chance of having sufficient time to accomplish what you need to get done if you do that first.

Too many conversations are held and decisions made because "We only have a few minutes left, and I know this is important…" If what you're working on is that important, give it the pride of place it deserves. You'll find people are more energetic, focused, and will feel like their time has been well spent.

Keep Attention, Get Good Input and Receive Quality Participation

If you ask almost anyone what their biggest concerns are when it comes to virtual meetings, they'll say keeping people involved, getting as many people as possible to contribute and keeping the attention of those who are merely observing or don't feel they have anything to contribute.

But when we blather on about people focusing and paying attention, what do we really mean? Usually it means they are thinking about, and doing, nothing other than what you as the meeting leader wants them to do at that exact moment in time. Good luck with that.

First, a word about "attention spans"

To be fair, people have a limited attention span at the best of times, and this isn't necessarily the best of times. Don't take it personally; meetings don't happen in a vacuum. There are plenty of things competing for their attention at any given time, and the odds that your meeting topic is their top priority are Bleak.

Think about what this "attention span" thing really is: it's the length of time a person is able to concentrate mentally on a particular activity. It's not completely a conscious choice…we are only able to concentrate our focus for a limited span. If your meeting pushes the boundaries of those limits, well, attention wanders. More often than not, it comes back eventually.

And there are plenty of distractions. Some are mental, like the pressures of looming deadlines for other tasks, or other demands on their time that make it hard to focus on the task at hand. Some are physical, like having a poor audio connection, which creates a physical strain on participants, or having to go to the bathroom (Seriously, Stalin, give them a break once in a while).

Some barriers to contribution are purely internal, like knowing you have to be on another meeting in 10 minutes. No five minutes….no, I'm late already arrrrrgggh, my boss is going to kill me…but I digress.

Other distractions are external and very real. Co-workers who won't leave them alone, or incoming email and instant messages. Even if they've turned off the incoming message notifications, the fear of what's in their inbox is real enough to take them off track.

The point is, we have finite attention to give. Don't feel bad if people sometimes wander or fade out. Hopefully they'll be back. On the other hand, if you know people don't have unlimited attention to offer, stop demanding it. Get down to the good stuff and help them.

The "Hrair Limit" and why it matters

One of the most important concepts I ever learned as a trainer has filtered down to most of my business life, including meetings. It's called the "Hrair Limit" (Google it—you'll find smarter people than me to explain it to you. It involves the book "Watership Down" and talking rabbits. Taking the time right now would, ironically, surpass your Hrair Limit.).

It's also known as the "Rule of 7", but essentially it describes a basic rule of human psychology: we take information into our short-term memory, then process it in multiple ways and move the important stuff into our long-term memory banks, dumping the rest overboard.

Studies have shown we can only take in an average of se
pieces of information before our short-term memory is full. Unless
process that information and turn it into something useable by askin
questions, applying the knowledge, saying it out loud and other
activities the storage is full...there's no room for new information.
This is why in a day-long meeting, you fight to stay focused, and your
brain feels full. It is full. And cramming more stuff into our brains
won't help you process it any better. In fact, it can make it worse
because we get so stressed about our losing focus that we lose our
focus even more.

So, if we're only wired to take in limited information before
needing to "do something with it", don't act so surprised that people
aren't riveted by every word or action that takes place. Your meeting
participants are only human. Plan your meetings accordingly.

If you've read this far in the book, we're going to assume that
you've made a good start of things:

- You invited people who actually have a stake in the outcome
  of the meeting or can add value to those who do.

- You provided them with an agenda that helps them focus
  their thinking and prepare to participate fully.

- You started the meeting by setting clear expectations of what
  the meeting will accomplish, why it matters, and how they're
  expected to participate.

- You've shared the tools that will make getting their input
  easy, and provided an opportunity to practice with them if
  necessary.

You've done a lot to make things better than they've been in the
past. In a sane universe your folks would be enthused, productive,
active and laser-focused. But as we all know, the world (at least the
parts involving work and webmeetings) ain't sane or even close to it.

You'll do yourself and them a huge favor by realizing where the
natural breaks are, and at what point people may be mentally stuffed,
then create opportunities to process, use and clarify the information
they take in.

BEST PRACTICE: Don't stress yourself out if people sometimes fade out, didn't hear the question or get caught daydreaming. It happens. First, you don't know what they're doing. Secondly, it might not mean your meeting is a disaster. It might mean they just need a potty break. Relax and do something to bring their focus back to the matter at hand like…

Identify logical activities that add value

As you look at your meeting agenda, you're probably thinking about how each item will be handled. Do you need to do a discussion and capture ideas on a whiteboard? Should you stop after each item and take questions or charge on through? I know the clock is ticking, but the right answer is usually not to charge on through.

What are some of the activities that will help people stay engaged and focused? They don't have to be very sophisticated:

- Call for questions and feedback.
- Use chat to make points and generate discussion.
- Use the "raise hands" and feedback features.
- Capture input and feedback with whiteboards.
- Incorporate polling and surveys.
- Use breakout rooms for small group discussions and report out to the whole group.
- Take breaks periodically. Believe they'll come back to you.

Remember, the trick is to add value and not simply do "busy work" in an attempt to keep people awake. They'll resent you wasting their time, and that will negatively impact the quality of your work together over time.

Once you've identified activities that will get people involved you have to remember to actually do them. This isn't obvious—when you're focused on getting through your agenda and the clock is ticking it's easy to forget to pause and ask questions, or just hear from the people who are willing to speak up.

Find a way to remind yourself to actively engage others. This be as invisible to participants as keeping a note pad on your compu next to your computer, or as obvious as putting a slide in you PowerPoint presentation to remind yourself to stop, encourage questions or input and involve the attendees.

Of course, the easiest way to hold yourself accountable is to tell everyone up front what to expect and let them keep your feet to the proverbial fire. When going over the meeting's agenda, don't just list topics. Explain how they can add value for each item.

It will give you a big old reminder not to just charge through the agenda. It'll also help your team plan their participation. And, if they are properly empowered, they'll even hold you responsible for following through.

Why don't people have questions when you ask, "Any questions?"

There is little more frustrating to meeting leaders than remembering to ask for input or questions, only to be met by deafening silence.

This is usually when we miss traditional meetings, because at least there you can make eye contact with someone and plead for them to speak up. Or you can simply stare at them til they speak out of a desire to break the uncomfortable silence. Sadly, we lack this option online.

There are several reasons for this silence, and only a couple of them are the result of malicious intent or lost attention. Here are just some of the reasons people don't have questions or input when you solicit it.

- They're answering email and didn't hear you.

- They did answer you, but the phone was on mute and by the time they realized it, they've given up.

- They want to ask, but are waiting for their turn, and by the time they decide to speak up, you've moved on. (Think about this one…in a meeting they can look around to see if someone else is going to speak. Online they don't have that option).

- They've tried a couple of times, but either someone else gets to speak first, or you interrupt them.

- They didn't understand the question.

- Every time they ask a question, someone on the team argues with them or creates drama. Who needs it?

- The clock is ticking, and time is almost up. If they ask questions, the meeting will just go longer.

- They figured at the speed you're moving, it was probably a rhetorical question and you don't really want their input.

- You never actually asked. Silence while pausing to catch your breath is not the same thing as actually asking for their input.

- They actually, legitimately don't have any questions.

There are some fairly simple reasons people don't ask questions or contribute to meetings: they're reluctant to speak up, they find speaking up more trouble than it's worth (socially or technologically) or they have nothing to contribute.

How can you ensure that people speak up and you hear from everyone? You need to have a strategy in place before the meeting starts, because if the meeting is running, it's hard to get creative about driving input.

Plan logical spots for questions and feedback

As with any kind of interaction and input, you want to identify logical breaks in the information or meeting where you can help people absorb what you're saying. Since we know that people can only take in so much information before they're completely overwhelmed, figure out where they might have questions or comments. Build in breaks and actively solicit their participation.

Also, plan how you'll take the questions:

- Do you want them to just speak up on the phone or audio? That's great for your extroverts, or people who are native English speakers, or those who actually are not worried about the quality of their phone lines. What about the rest of y team?

- How many people do you have on the line? Maybe writter chat or the Q and A box are the best way to go? (Check out the Features section for more on this)

- Identify someone to be your co-pilot. They can keep an eye on the chat and Question box so that you can concentrate on what you're doing.

BEST PRACTICE: Most people are not used to interactive online meetings. They're more used to leaders paying lip service to participation while actively discouraging it. Hold yourself and your team accountable by generating questions and input as early in the meeting as possible so they know you mean it.

Plan to ask three types of questions

When we lead meetings online, we often forget a lot of the basic facilitation skills that we use (or should be using, that's between you and your conscience) all the time in face-to-face settings.

For example, asking a question like "Does that make sense?" often sounds like a rhetorical question and no one volunteers a response. If you're legitimately looking for input, that can be deadly. What you need to do is have a questioning strategy in place before you fire up GoToMeeting, WebEx or LiveMeeting (or whichever tool you use).

There are at least three types of questions you should be asking:

- **"Anyone" type questions.** These are also known as "overhead" questions. You just throw them out and hope someone answers them. The good news is that you should be able to get lots of input. The problem is it's often from the same people all the time. Again, you sometimes are met with silence. First, remind them that these are NOT rhetorical questions and you expect an answer. Don't be afraid of silence. They may need time to think (heaven forbid someone think about an answer) or even to unmute their phone before anyone can hear them.

- **"Someone we haven't heard from" questions.** As the leader, you often have to direct the conversational traffic. If you're hearing from the same people over and over, the introverts and the less confident will be left out. This will also help the people on the line who are rolling their eyes when someone starts to hijack the conversation.

- **"Directed" questions.** In smaller meetings, don't be afraid to call on people by name. Sometimes this will be because you know they have valuable insight. Sometimes it will be just to make sure they're not answering email or telling everyone on Twitter how miserable they are. Either way, you have to be aware of the dynamics of the meeting and facilitate everyone's participation.

BEST PRACTICE: It's all too easy to fall into a pattern of using the same type of questions. Usually it's the "Anyone?" question. Make a note to yourself of who you've heard from, and who you haven't. Are there people you especially want to hear from during a particular discussion? Find a way to make it happen. Better it be a little forced, than to try to make it happen organically and not have the outcome you most want.

Good meeting facilitation, in person or online, doesn't happen by accident. Having these three types of questions in mind, and using them properly, will help increase the return on investment for your team's time and energy.

Here are a couple of other things to consider about your questioning strategy.

It's okay to call on people. Really. Just don't be a bully about it.

If one of our biggest complaints is that people don't particip why don't we just expect them to chime in? Sometimes it's said don't offer enough opportunity to contribute. Other times, there ample opportunity, but people don't take advantage. Often there's nc comfortable way to hold people accountable for their input.

Leading a meeting is an act of leadership. It's not easy, and it's not for the faint of heart. Neither is being a productive member of the team. You need to get input when you don't particularly want to hear it and hold people accountable for their input when they aren't forthcoming as quickly as we'd like.

I don't want to be a Philistine, here, but maybe we're just gun shy. Somehow it's become a rule of thumb that you never put anyone on the spot or call on them by name. This is simply an overreaction to bosses who love to ask questions to demonstrate how much the people in the meeting don't know, or to embarrass people for whatever reason.

Accountability is okay, shame is not something you want to encourage (although my Canadian grandmother will tell you it's the only thing that'll keep some people on the straight and narrow. Discuss amongst yourselves...)

Here are a couple of rules to call on people without being a jerk:

- Tell them at the outset you expect everyone's participation then hold them to it.

- Call on people you haven't heard from when you think there's a very good chance that they have a strong opinion or questions based on past conversations or communication. If you know that Mary is concerned about an issue, and you haven't heard from her, it's your job to solicit her feedback. Maybe she understands and says, "No, I'm fine". Great, she had her chance and your conscience is clear.

- Warn them you expect to hear from someone new. Start your question with a preamble designed to get their attention: "Let's hear from someone we haven't heard from yet..." or "The IT group in Dallas has been awfully quiet. I'm sure you have some concerns..."

Remember; the goal is to encourage participation and hold people accountable, not to play "gotcha" and catch people napping. Of course, that may happen occasionally but it should be an occasional occurrence, not part of your master plan. One is an unintended consequence of interactive meetings, the other is just creepy.

An unnecessary but heart felt idea here: try to avoid being a jerk. That may be part of the problem with how people act in your meetings in the first place.

Conversation isn't always auditory- writing counts too

One of the great things about webmeetings over traditional conference calls is the ability to share information in a number of ways. Don't underestimate that capability or, worse, choke it off for fear of inconvenience.

Some of your folks; the shy, the overly polite, the frustrated, the English limited, may want to contribute but aren't comfortable doing so by speaking up. There's no reason not to leverage the power of these tools.

Just make sure you set the rules, and have a way to comfortably screen the content. A co-pilot is really helpful here.

BEST PRACTICE: Use the private chat to encourage input from people. I find that some people need a nudge to speak up, especially if they're not sure of the reaction or know it could be unpopular. A private chat message like, "George, you mentioned you had some concerns about this…" or "Rajesh, you were at that conference, what did you think? We'd love to hear it…" is a great way to encourage people to participate and share their concerns, thoughts, and wisdom.

Communicating privately also prevents one of the great fears unintended frustrations of webmeetings: calling on someone wh stepped away from their computer or is having technical trouble. Whe you call on someone who is unprepared, or isn't even there, it slows things down and makes them or you look foolish and unprepared. Here's where it's easy to cross over into jerk territory.

Your job doesn't stop when the meeting does

The fact remains that past experience is still the best indicator of future performance. If virtual meetings in the past have been awful and unproductive, one well-run meeting won't change people's attitudes, expectations, and opinions. To really effect change, you need to have consistently good meetings over time.

This means you have to continue to lead your meetings well, even when they don't seem to be getting the results you want. It may also mean you need to have coaching conversations with individuals. If you have people who are extremely vocal or concerned privately, but don't speak up on meetings, there's probably a compelling reason.

A follow up call with those individuals is probably in order. Call, not email. Maybe you want to talk to them as soon as the meeting is over. Or you can put it on the top of your list of things to discuss during your one-on-one time. Either way, you need to find out what's getting in the way of their participation and remove real or perceived barriers to their full participation.

As a leader, particularly a project or team leader, you need to find out what's happening now and set expectations for the future. It might not save this meeting, but will bear fruit in the future. Anyone can say they want full participation. It's something else entirely to run your meetings like you mean it.

Ending the Meeting and Following Up

If "Well begun is half done", as Mary Poppins (or whoever it was) said, badly ended undoes all the good stuff you've done. That one's all mine—and while it lacks poetry, it's all too true.

There are a few things that make for a good ending to a meeting:

- It ends on time, or close enough to it. Maybe even early, who knows?

- The stated goals are met, and the desired outcomes actually come out.

- The work people put into the meeting (whether that's research, participation or just getting answers to their questions) is rewarded.

- They know what's next in their work.

- They know who is expected to do what next (and have reasonable faith it will happen).

- There's a reasonable expectation the next meeting will be as productive as this one.

Managing Time

We'd like to think that meetings that start on time and end on time are well-run. To a degree that's true, but what really matters is what happens between sign on and log off. We've already discussed how to get your meetings started on time, so let's focus on wrapping them up in a timely manner.

The first thing about managing the time is having a realistic agenda. Can you actually accomplish everything you set out to do? If not, you've set yourself up for failure and you're doomed to disappoint those who put their faith in your meeting leadership. Not to be a downer about it, but you've just confirmed their worst suspicions about how these things go. Not exactly what you were looking for, was it?

One way to ease the frustration of running out of time is to focus on the agenda rather than the timeline. How much time you allot for a discussion or topic should depend on how critical it is to your desired outcomes. It's based on the priority you and your participants assign to it.

To quote Johnny Depp in Pirates of the Caribbean, "It's not so much code as it is guidelines".

If it helps to get all metaphysical, time is an artificial construct. It means what we want it to mean. In practical terms, you've noticed that sometimes people say they have an hour but tune out almost immediately. Other times, they say they only have ten minutes but will stay engaged for much longer. The lesson, in that case, is that time is flexible, and people are really good at stretching it if they're interested in what's happening.

They will give you all day if it's in their power and they actually care about what's going on.

Here are some tips for managing time effectively:

- Check in with your team at the beginning of the meeting. Are there items people aren't prepared, or even want, to tackle during this meeting? If so, just remove them now and free up room. Do people have hard deadlines? Does everyone have to leave the meeting at the same time? Move the items that require hearing from everyone to a place on the agenda where everyone (or at least as many as practical) can take part and add value.

- Get buy-in to the original timeline when the meeting starts. Help people set expectations and plan to stick to timelines as best they can.

- As the original time nears its end, check with your participants. Have you accomplished what you've set out to do? Is there more to discuss? In this way, you can move on early from topics that have exhausted themselves and gain some more time.

- Re-prioritize throughout the meeting. What are the things that are either time-sensitive or critical to your overall project timeline? Items on the critical path have priority over the items you'll have to discuss "eventually".

- Can the information be transmitted asynchronously? If you're merely handing out reports, or sending monthly updates, ask if you really need to take time together that could be spent on issues requiring real-time input. Spend time where it will do the most good. Making them available by file transfer or email might be just as useful.

- Assign someone to watch the time for you. This can be a formal arrangement or just ask someone to private message you to quit yacking and watch the clock. Better yet, empower everyone to speak up if they feel time's awasting. And take time to check with everyone periodically.

BEST PRACTICE: Whatever methods you use to manage time in your meetings, do them transparently. It's important that you not only mind people's time, but that you're seen doing it. People need to know that you and the team care about getting the work done and respect the time and efforts of the people doing that work. Maybe it won't matter much at first. Maybe they'll smirk and assume that "this, too, shall pass". But over time it will be trust and a culture of respect for time and a focus on getting real wo. done.

Wrap up and let them know "The End is near"

Most meetings, in person or online, tend to end rather suddenly and go out with a whimper rather than a bang. We try to cram every possible minute or work we can possibly squeeze in before announcing, "Okay, we're out of time… "and let people scatter to the winds. Most people mentally check out at that point, and never hear, nor participate in, the wrap up of the meeting.

Do they hear and agree to the action items, deadlines and next steps? Or are they too busy packing up, closing down and mentally moving on to their next meeting? More importantly, do they hear you congratulate them on their successes and celebrate their successes?

You're doing all that stuff, right?

Remember our goals. Not only do we want to accomplish the work for this meeting, but we need to set the groundwork for successful future meetings, collaboration and task completion. We need to drive the work forward. That's awfully hard to do in the last five minutes of a meeting as people are already Googling the traffic home.

You need to plan your ending and give yourself time to do it in a way that positions you for success.

Pick an arbitrary amount of time before the scheduled end of the meeting to do a check-in with your participants. Ten minutes is about right, but you can look for a logical place to break.

At that point you'll want to make sure you:

- Announce the time and time left.
- Celebrate what you've accomplished so far.
- Refer to the agenda. What remains to be done (if anything)?
- Take the pulse of the audience. Are they still with you? What's left on the agenda that needs to be accomplished?

- Get agreement on what still needs to be done, and what can or should be tabled for the next meeting. If you can wrap up your important work in a few more minutes, can they hang in there and finish up? Hear from everyone with a stake in the outcome and get explicit permission to continue.

- Get back to work and finish up. You've got stuff to do.

Invest time in a good wrap up.

The time you spend in your wrap up is well invested. The problem is you want everyone else invested as well. The close of your meeting shouldn't be an afterthought. Nor should it be only the responsibility of the meeting leader.

Closing the meeting involves wrapping up the task at hand, getting buy-in and agreement on action items and next steps. Maybe most importantly, it involves commitment to applying that new information to the work at hand.

That's hard to do when you're already dialing in to your next teleconference or on a cell phone heading to the car to beat traffic.

Here's how to conduct a good wrap up.

- Announce that you're wrapping up now.
- Refer back to the original purpose and outcome of the meeting. Did you accomplish your goals? If not, did you at least come close or make progress?
- Call for feedback on whether participants agree. If not, why not?
- Celebrate success and acknowledge work to be done.
- Go through action items and next steps. If you've been keeping a running list on a whiteboard, share it now. Encourage participants to save the list to their computers so there is no confusion.
- Review the action item list.

- Get verbal agreement on action items from the responsible party. If Rajesh is to get the report out to everyone by Tuesday, everyone wants to hear her say that.

BEST PRACTICE: Don't just ask if someon. knows they have an action item. You'll most likely get a "yes" that might be real agreement, or might just be a way of making you go away and leave them alone.

Instead, when pointing out an action item, follow it up with the question, "What do you need to make this deadline, and how can we help?" Don't let it go until you get an answer. If they need help from other teammates, or there's an obstacle in the way, you're more likely to get an honest answer from a direct, open-ended question.

- Ask if there are any additions to the list you may have missed. Actively seek input.

- Preview the next meeting. Are there action items that need to be carried over? Should people start preparing?

- Thank them for their participation. If there were particularly notable contributions, highlight those contributions in a positive way.

- What could be done better for next time? For example, if more people need to come prepared, don't be afraid to mention that point. You don't have to call out individuals, merely state that the people who came prepared need help from their peers.

- Give people a chance for any last minute requests or comments.

- Remind them again how the work you've done today will impact their work going forward. Make a direct connection to show them their time hasn't been spent—it's been invested.

Send them off to work feeling good about themselves, their work, and you as a meeting leader.

After the meeting…

Just because you've logged off the webmeeting, doesn't mean your work is complete. You need to do some very specific things to keep the momentum going and plant seeds for continued success.

First, build into your schedule about 15 minutes after the planned wrap-up time. What are you going to do with that time?

Save everything from that meeting in a file. This can be on your computer or in a shared file where everyone can access it. When we say "everything" what do we mean?

- Save any files used in the meeting. This includes PowerPoints, documents, whiteboards, chat logs, surveys or other records of the meeting.

- If you recorded the meeting, save that recording in the same place.

Next, think about the people in the meeting. You know that feedback loses impact over time. You need to reach out and thank those who made special contributions, and plan to coach those who didn't contribute, or exhibited behavior that was less than constructive. Don't wait to do this.

Maybe it's a quick email thanking someone for a particularly good piece of feedback. Perhaps you just want to thank them for speaking up when that's not something that normally happens.

Or perhaps you need to talk to Mary about her tendency to interrupt or belittle others when they're contributing. This isn't something you should put in an email. If you don't have time to give her that feedback at that exact moment, at least get on her calendar to speak soon.

If the next meeting is going to be better than this one, you'll need to reinforce the positive behavior and address things that didn't work. As a leader, you need to step up.

Finally, take a look at the meeting evaluation questionnaire you looked at in the first chapter. Was your meeting successful? What could you as the meeting leader have done differently or better?

What help do you need to ensure that the next meeting is better than this one? Who can you reach out to? What resources do need?

Be specific about what you need to do and take action.

There, now you're done.

Section 5:
Some Meeting Formats You Might Want to Try

"Whenever you are asked if you can do a job, tell 'em, Certainly I can! Then get busy and find out how to do it."

Theodore Roosevelt

Virtual Meeting Formats and Techniques That Get Results

Let's start this section with an obvious statement: Good people can run some really bad meetings. We're going to assume that you are a good person, and we'll go out on a limb and also assume (since you sprung for this book, and you're unlikely to be a relative of mine or buying it out of pity) that your meetings occasionally go astray and you want to do something about that.

The reason that meetings so often go off the rail is that there's a ton going on. It's really difficult to run the technology, listen and facilitate effectively, remember who's contributed and who hasn't, and watch the clock so you can get everything done on time. Actually, when you look at it, it's almost more surprising so many of us actually function on a daily basis.

One thing I've found helpful in my career is to have some kind of structure which almost automates certain processes. If you follow step by step, it's easier to stay on track and harder to forget steps or important information. It's not that you want to be so in lock-step that your meetings lack humanity, but it gives you the best chance to generate the best outcomes and get your team's work done.

There have been entire books written on meeting techniques, and you can find lots more information on these and others. The idea here is to help you identify formats that are aimed at project teams and lend themselves to maximizing your virtual meeting tools.

Here are four meeting formats you may not have used, or even heard of, but they may add value to the time you invest in your virtual meetings.

1   Root Cause Analysis

This is really a form of brainstorming in that you are trying to gather as much information as possible before actually seeking a solution.

When to use this format

Ever spend time brainstorming a solution to a problem, only find out you're solving the wrong problem? Put your hand down, it's rhetorical question.

In fact, we've all done it. It wastes time and builds on the backlog of resentment and lost faith your team might have in you and in each other.

This is a great technique to use when you need to take a deep breath and understand what's really going on with a situation. Maybe most importantly, this process gets input from everyone in a systematic way and captures the information so that it can be displayed graphically and stored for future reference.

How it works

The conversation starts with the notion that the real cause of a problem lays in at least one of several areas:

- People
- Processes
- Resources
- Location/Site
- Policies

This is only the most common example. There are other areas that can be included in different cases. Sometimes you need to include clients or cultural considerations. Before launching into your problem-solving session, ensure that everyone is in agreement on the areas to be examined.

This type of discussion uses a graphic format often called a "fishbone" diagram. That's because it looks like the stripped skeleton of a (rather odd looking) fish with the "bones" representing each of the areas you need to investigate.

You then get input from as many people as possible on potential sources of the problem(s). What are some of the people problems causing the issue? Is paperwork or other process problems creating difficulty?

Here's one that's started. Notice you can use the simple annotation tools on the whiteboard:

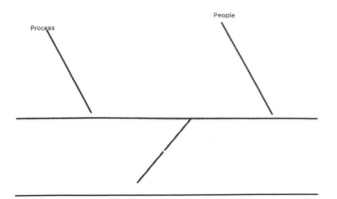

Capture the ideas on a virtual whiteboard as they arise. Remember you can enlist the help of others to write on the board so you can manage the process.

You can tackle this any way you'd like. If it makes sense to start with each of the problem areas, knock yourself out. Maybe you prefer to go from person to person in "round robin" fashion. It really doesn't matter, and here's why…

The important thing to remember (and here's why the graphic reminder is so critical to this process) is that people don't think linearly or in an orderly fashion. While someone is listing the reason the problem lies with people, someone else is looking at the whiteboard and another idea comes to mind, or they think, "Hey, what about that enlistment process…that's where the real problem is".

Keep going around the group until you've exhausted any ideas people may have. Don't be surprised if ideas keep popping up as you have the ongoing discussion. Just get them down. Maybe they're relevant, maybe not. You won't know until you put them down and discuss them.

When everyone has taken the chance to contribute their ideas, it's time to start paring down. Start moving through the ideas. Check that everyone understands what each contribution means. Is it relevant? If it's not relevant, feel free to cross it off or erase it.

Use chat or voice to examine each possibility and hear everyone.

How to maximize the virtual tools

The most obvious tool to use for this conversation is the whiteboard tool. It creates a dynamic visual to generate discussion and capture input. You can then cross out, erase, or move information as it arises and is appropriate.

You can use colors and various annotation tools to write, highlight, or create visual interest in your information

Input can come by voice or chat, and the more input the better.

One really important way to maximize the information is to allow everyone to download or copy the whiteboard for themselves. No more transcribing and emailing. Nothing is open to misinterpretation when the original document is right there at everyone's disposal.

Best tips

There are several best practices for this meeting format:

- **Don't assume that everything has to be solved in one meeting.** Often you'll generate more thoughtful input and can hear from people who couldn't attend the original meeting by doing the brainstorming in one session. Then you can actually address those results in another, subsequent meeting. You can give people time to think about what you might have missed, digest and process the information and be ready to really dig into a solution if you give them time to think

- **Allow the ideas to flow freely.** If you ask for input on "process" and someone has a thought about "people", let it rip. The point is to get as much input as you can and narrow it down from there.

- **Everyone should contribute.** If they have the same idea as someone else, demonstrate that by using a checkmark or other stamp tool. Sometimes you'll see consensus develop visually as you go but...

- **...Don't assume that the majority is right.** Often the obvious answer isn't the most logical or even the right one. Complete the entire process before deciding that you've identified the root cause.

2   Nominal Group Technique

This technique was designed back in the '60s and is used very often to help create consensus in a group. It's a very democratic process, but the results tend to get you better answers than a straight vote or show of hands. It's also very effective for making sure everyone is heard from.

It requires practice, and can feel very formal. The results tend to be worth the effort though, and it goes a long way to helping teams bond over a solution and hit the ground running.

When to use this format

To be honest, this is a great format to use when the solution you need to come up with needs buy-in from the greatest number of people. If you need the "most correct" answer, it may not work as the results tend to favor everyone being able to live with the results.

Amazingly enough, that is good enough for most situations. Not everyone needs to win every battle, and by getting as much input as possible, the team will have great insight into how everyone thinks, and where they place their priorities.

How it works

As with most brainstorming techniques, there are three basic steps to this kind of meeting. First, you have to generate ideas. Then distill them down to the best ideas or groups of ideas. Finally select the best answer -- or at least the answer most people can feel comfortable with.

Each step requires some rigor, strong leadership and good use of the virtual tools to get maximum results from your team. It also presumes you're asking the right questions, because you WILL come up with an answer, and people will expect it to be implemented. You'd best not disappoint them.

Step 1: Generating Ideas

One of the biggest challenges with this meeting technique is r generating ideas, it's generating ideas that are focused on the questio at hand. You also want to make sure everyone is heard from in turn.

The best way to start is by putting the question up on a PowerPoint slide or whiteboard. Ask the question the way you want it answered. "How do we increase revenue?" is one question and will get you a set of answers very different from "How do we increase revenue in our existing client base?"

Take the time to get buy-in to the question you're asking. Does everyone understand the desired outcome? Are they clear on the constraints? You will often be amazed at the divergent thinking on exactly what a single sentence means. Just accept it, and try not to let your exasperation show. That's why you make the big bucks.

Once everyone is clear on what they are trying to accomplish, it's time to come up with ideas. Give people time in silence to ponder their contributions. Somewhere between 5 and 10 minutes is about right, depending on how familiar they are with the situation you're trying to address and the amount of thought they've given to it.

Not to be a nag, but it will help them come prepared to do battle if you've told them in the agenda what you'll discuss and the desired outcome. If they are prepared, great. An extra couple of minutes to put the ideas in writing will help them be clear and concise. If they weren't prepared, they now have 10 minutes or so to contribute and have no excuse for not contributing.

When time is up, call on each individual to tell you what they came up with. At this point you're going for quantity of ideas, you'll refine them later.

The order in which you take ideas is up to you, but it's often a not a good idea to start with your strongest personalities or influencers Depending on your group's dynamics it may intimidate others or cause them to self-edit perfectly good ideas.

Capture all the ideas on a whiteboard or a shared Word Document (I prefer the editing and sharing abilities of the whiteboard but it depends on the tool you use). People can cut and paste their own ideas, or you can use a partner to capture and write the ideas down.

Step 2: Discuss and distill

When you have captured and displayed everyone's ideas, it's time to boil them down to a usable number, but this will require some input and discussion. The first step is to make sure you understand what people mean by what they've said.

Go through the list. Ask the person who came up with that idea to discuss it in more depth. Does it require more explanation or clarification? This means everyone has a chance to defend or at least clarify their thinking.

You'll often find that a number of people have contributed the same idea. They may call it different things (one person's "revenue generation" is another persons' "sales") but if it's the same idea, group them together, or eliminate duplicates. Some platforms will allow you to drag and drop items to different parts of the whiteboard to make this simpler.

Eventually you'll eliminate duplicate ideas and wind up with a whiteboard with a number of suggestions. Don't eliminate them just because they sound silly. Only eliminate duplicates and obvious smart-aleck answers so you're working with a good selection of answers with lots of white space and room to maneuver.

You'll be tempted to spend most of your time on the idea generation and treat this distillation process as something to do quickly and get out of the way. Actually, this is where the good discussion comes from. Encourage people to ask questions, and if more details aren't forthcoming ask them yourself.

"How exactly do you see that happening?" or "What does that look like in your mind?" are good "fire-starter" type questions.

The point here is to really help people define their ideas, share them with the team, and in the process of answering you'll find the ideas morph and even create new ideas. Add them to the list and keep going.

It's important to keep your tone neutral. You will obviously h. a sense of what you'd like to do—but that's not the point of the exercise. If people feel that all this hard work is only to rubberstamp what the leadership (or the Company, or Big Brother, depending on the general feeling) wants to do anyway you'll lose all the good will you've built up.

One great way to do this is to use the PIN technique (you'll read about it in just a bit). This forces you to say something nice about every idea and not push your agenda.

Step 3: Choose an option

Eventually the time comes when everyone's had their say. Conversation starts to go in circles, points are rehashed again and again. When this happens meetings often start to drag and people begin to tune out. When you get the feeling that what's been said is sufficient to allow discussion but not too repetitive, it's actually time for the group or team to make a decision. After all, that's why you're all there.

You might decide to vote by rank or by rating. The differences are subtle but the outcome is the same: everybody has to spread their votes across several options. This means while the group may not choose their first choice, they probably have some level of agreement with what your team ultimately decides. This helps develop buy-in (since you've demonstrated can live with one of the other options) and the process has been transparent to all.

Here's how the voting actually works: every individual gets to look at the options on the board and choose the answers or solutions they like best in order of first choice to last. Assuming you have more than five possible solutions on the board, the voting occurs this way:

- **If you're ranking options** everyone has the opportunity to choose the options from one (their absolute best or favorite solution) to five (or three if there are fewer options). Use the annotation tools to visually display the answers as they arise. The solution with the highest ranking is the group's choice.

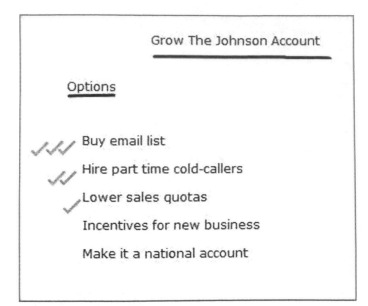

Grow The Johnson Account

Options

Buy email list

Hire part time cold-callers

Lower sales quotas

Incentives for new business

Make it a national account

- **If you're "rating" options the** process works very much the same way except that everyone has a finite number of points up to the number of options you have displayed. They can then distribute those points across the spectrum of answers. The answers they feel most strongly about would get the most points. For example, if there are six options to choose from, someone may give their first choice three points, their second choice two points and a third choice one point. Someone else may not feel so strongly and give an equal number of votes to several, or even all, of the options. Total the number of points awarded to each solution and there's your winner.

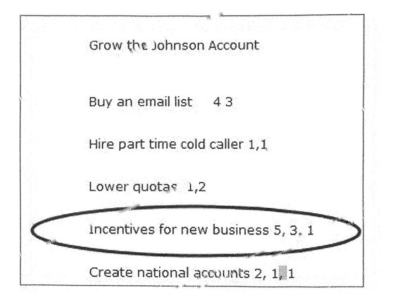

Grow the Johnson Account

Buy an email list   4 3

Hire part time cold caller 1,1

Lower quotas 1,2

Incentives for new business 5, 3. 1

Create national accounts 2, 1. 1

There are a couple of things to keep in mind when running these types of events. Remember the idea is to get buy-in to the solution.

First, if you have a lot of options to choose from, the possible solutions may be closely scored. If there is no clear winner, try eliminating the lowest scoring alternatives and having a second vote. This technique forces people to actively choose a solution that is viable.

Secondly, the idea is to take action on whatever is chosen. This requires commitment from everyone, even those who may have been opposed to the idea. When the voting is over, get verbal or chat commitment from everyone to the solution. Ask clearly, "Can you support this solution?"

You will want to both hold people accountable for their participation going forward (they voted for this!) and identify areas of real resistance both now and down the road.

How to maximize the virtual tools

The tools in your webmeeting platform are really helpful for these types of meetings. They allow both public and private input, and displays options and actions visually, which increases transparency and accountability. The numbers don't lie.

Tools you should consider using for these types of discussions:

- Public and private chat lets you to prompt for feedback when necessary.

- Whiteboards allow people to insert their own options and encourages activity in the discussion. If you're happy with that, great. If not have someone act as your scribe.

- Polling or survey tools can help with ranking the answers (assuming they allow for multiple answers).

- Annotation tools can make the voting process graphically interesting, colorful, and engaging.

- Record the voting if you feel a permanent record of the session is important.

- Save the whiteboard and any other tools and allow others to save them to their computers as documented proof of the outcomes.

BEST PRACTICE: Depending on the timing, importance, and scope of the decision to be made, you may want to spread the voting over two meetings. You can get suggested answers in advance to start the conversation, but people may not have done their homework or couldn't make the meeting, or get an idea based on the discussion while it's happening. Additionally, people may have great "in the shower" ideas after the original meeting. Give them time to submit new answers and have the actual voting occur in a subsequent session.

3   SWOT Analysis

Sometimes a discussion is more important than making a single, actionable decision. You need to create context and understanding for the work you're doing together. As a group you need to understand what's going on in the business or your project team and get everyone's best thinking.

What you need is a way to frame the discussion, make sure discuss and capture what's really important, and don't disconnect fro the meeting thinking, "Shoot, I forgot to talk about _____",

SWOT stands for Strengths, Weaknesses, Opportunities and Threats. Sometimes the issues you're trying to address just seem overwhelming, and the conversation meanders all over. What this format does, is create a framework to guide the discussion. It makes sure all the important factors are considered in a methodical way.

When to use this format

Too often, your meetings become free-for-all discussions. The same individuals dominate, and everyone leaves the meeting not really sure what was accomplished or what's next. By running a good SWOT meeting, everyone will be up to speed on a given situation and have the opportunity for input.

Often the documents and saved whiteboards become critical to action planning and future meetings so you want to make sure they're capturing the critical information.

How it works

SWOT meetings work the same way virtually as they do in a conference room. Use a whiteboard or Word Doc to methodically work through the discussion and capture key information.

Whether you call on volunteers or go person by person, don't give anyone the excuse that their input wasn't solicited or expected. Set good ground rules and expectations and hold people accountable.

Let's say you want to figure out your sales strategy for next year, or what your new upgraded software version should look like? You want to go step by step in an orderly fashion. Capture ideas on the whiteboard as you go.

You can start with a single whiteboard broken into four quadrants, or one whiteboard per topic, depending on how detailed the conversation will be. Do take them in this order.

Starting with the positive is often a good way to overcome rampant negativity. After all, something is working and it's not all bleak. It will also calm down the more emotional members of the team who may tend to be in panic mode. Start with the positive and get to the hard stuff later.

Strengths: Humans have a tendency to focus on the negative, and solutions often throw the proverbial baby out with the bathwater. Help people maintain a positive attitude by acknowledging the good in a situation. It's also important to recognize what's working and shouldn't change as you look to a solution.

What's working well? What metrics are being met or surpassed? What is critical to your company or team's culture that you want to maintain? Capture all this information and document it. Depending on the mood of your team, visual proof that there is good in all this is a morale-booster.

Weaknesses: One of the hardest things about leading SWOT meetings is not bogging down here. It's easy to get sucked into whining and complaining. Keep the conversation moving. Also, keep the items you discuss and record specific. "We don't have enough good leads" is a specific, legitimate weakness for purposes of the discussion. "Marketing sucks" is not specific. (True or not, it's not really actionable).

Opportunities: This is the chance to get really creative. What would the solution or new product do or solve? What could it look like in a perfect world? This might be a difficult idea for some people, and you'll have to be encouraging and positive. Encourage brainstorming and crazy ideas.

Threats: These are the factors or details that are driving the change or action. It also includes forces that might constrain your possible solution or action. What's going on that could impact your team, product or project? These can be internal (upcoming budget challenges) or external (seems the market for VHS cassettes isn't what it once was. Who knew?).

Getting all these out on the table accomplishes a number things. It creates a sense of urgency to solve the problem or ta action. It informs all team members of the reality of the situation (an it's amazing how often people don't have a realistic, big picture view of your business) and what constraints will be put on a possible solution.

Don't get bogged down in the details or attempt to prioritize as you go. When you've got everything captured, you can go back and separate the important from the trivial, and the mildly annoying from the critical.

When you're done you should have a clear, candid and detailed picture of what you're trying to address, what a possible solution should look like, and what constraints may help or hinder your attempts to move forward.

Everyone should have contributed to this discussion. Some people will finally have a chance to be heard. Some will be stunned into silence because they had no idea of what conditions or constraints they've been dealing with.

The point is, when you're done people should understand the depth and gravity of the situation, as well as what great ideas or possibilities offer light at the end of the tunnel.

How to maximize the virtual tools

Basically, any of the webmeeting tools that allow for maximum participation and input are fair game here. Tools you should consider using for these types of discussions:

- **Public and private chat.** Give people input and don't be afraid to nudge them privately if they're not forthcoming.

- **Whiteboard.** If you want people to insert their own options, great. If not, have someone act as your scribe. You might want to use one full whiteboard per topic. This could take a while and have a lot of information you want to capture for posterity (and future meetings).

- **Annotation tools** can make the voting process graphically interesting, colorful, and engaging.

- **Record the voting** if you feel a permanent record of the session is important.

- **Save the whiteboard** and any other tools and allow others to save them to their computers as documented proof of the outcomes.

BEST PRACTICE: Because you want to make sure you exhaust each topic, as well as not get caught up in negativity and whining, you want to take these in order and one at a time. Unfortunately, our minds seldom work that way. If someone makes a contribution that belongs in another category—let's say you're discussing Opportunities and someone identifies a Threat—the meeting or discussion leader (and it doesn't have to be you, you know) should simply write it on the appropriate whiteboard to be discussed later.

4   PIN Technique

Have you ever been in a meeting and offered your thoughts, only to have them shot down as soon as they leave your mouth? It happens too often. Frequently this creates an environment where people don't feel comfortable offering input or ideas. PIN is a facilitation technique that's designed to prevent criticism that can shut down input.

PIN stands for Positive, Interesting and Negative. Basically, it's how to offer feedback in a way that acknowledges the positive in someone's contribution before stating any problems with that idea.

Note that positive feedback is not the same as an absence of negative. You and your team want to truly look at the good in a solution. Phrases like "What I like about it is…" or "That might work because…" are real positive feedback. "That idea isn't the stupidest thing I've ever heard" is not, no matter how hard you try to spin it.

When to use this format

Leaders can use this concept any time you want to encourage honest input and postpone judgment. Implementing it as the way your team offers feedback can go a long way to building a culture of respect and inclusion.

Generally, it can be used as part of any general brainstorming session. It can also act as part of one of the sessions mentioned above. When examining options for a Nominal Group meeting, applying PIN to the discussion can help create objective discussion with fewer negative influences.

This idea should be explained and agreed to when you're about to go into discussions that require evaluation and feedback. Get everyone's agreement that this is how discussions will be handled before launching into the discussion.

How it works

Like so much in life (and leadership) there's a difference between simple and easy. This is a simple tool to lead discussions. It's also hard to remember when the heat's on.

Essentially you start any discussion of an idea or contribution with the Positive. What about the idea works? What might work under the right conditions? What would it address?

Make your contributions here complete sentences. You'll negate any positive feedback you give with "I like that idea because it will save us money, but it'll never work because…". There will be plenty of time to say why something is a bad idea.

The next, and most overlooked step, is to examine the interesting aspects of an idea. These are the ideas or suggestions which are unclear or not fully formed. Maybe someone's idea won't work because of safety regulations, but if you could do it in a way that meets local bylaws it has potential.

Seldom do answers arrive fully formed. Often someone says something and it's built upon, questioned and strengthened by additions from the rest of the team. It's amazing how many good, creative ideas are smothered at birth because people don't dig into the potential of an idea.

Digging into the interesting aspects of a suggestion or comment will reap great benefits. It's also the part that usually gets overlooked because we tend to look at ideas as either good or bad, workable or impossible. The good stuff often lies in between the two extremes. Leaders and teams often overlook this step because it's so much easier to just get to the negative.

Saving negative feedback for the end is an important step in team communication. First of all, you tend to be more careful about what you say. Blurting out the first thought that comes into your head can lead to hurt feelings. By pausing before saying why an idea won't work, you may actually be forced to evaluate it on its strengths, rather than by your first reaction to it.

It's important to make sure you're focusing your feedback on the negative points of the suggestion, and not on the person presenting the idea. "That won't work, and here's why…" is different feedback from "You always ignore the facts…". One piece of feedback is about the idea itself, the other is about the person.

By slowing down the conversation, making people acknowledge the Positive and Interesting aspects of an idea before the negative creates an environment where everyone's ideas are judged fairly, and people are forced to examine their first responses to ideas and input. That's not a bad set of rules for most conversations, not just team meetings.

How to maximize the virtual tools

This is less of a mechanical technique requiring specific tools than it is a mindset. The best way to enforce PIN feedback is for the meeting leader to set the ground rules in advance of the discussion. If it helps, visual reinforcement can come in the shape of PIN written on the whiteboard or a PPT slide.

BEST PRACTICE: Explain the concept before the discussion begins in earnest. Modeling it and holding people accountable is even more critical. That's not a function of technology, but your meeting leadership.

Practice this technique when coaching your participants and don
be afraid to interrupt a discussion while it's in progress. If someone is
going negative before acknowledging the positive aspects, interject
with a question: "Mary, I understand your concerns, but what about
Dave's idea might work…?"

A Quick Note About Hybrid Meetings

Up until now, we've made the assumption that the meetings
you're holding are either in-person, live events, or connected virtually
through WebEx or some similar software. However, as with most
assumptions, that may not be the reality of the situation.

Many of us hold meetings that are not completely one or the
other. Usually this involves a bunch of people sitting around a
conference room speakerphone while one or more team members are
connected virtually by webcams or just the phone.

The challenges are numerous, but the most common complaints
about these hybrid meetings are:

- The people on the other end feel excluded from the
  proceedings.

- They aren't there to hear the jokes. Often they hear an
  incoherent mumble, followed by laughter. Even when you're
  trying not to make people feel excluded, it happens.

- Unless they are particularly insistent they don't feel
  comfortable contributing to your meeting as often as they
  would if they were in the room.

- Because meeting leaders take their visual cues from the
  people in the room, it's easy to forget people connected
  remotely are trying to participate fully. We tend to take the
  first comments and questions from the people we can see. All
  the good questions are asked by the time you remember to
  ask, "What about the rest of you?"

There are two best practices I like to put in place to ensure that
these meetings (which, let's face it, will never be optimal) don't have to
be as ineffective as they usually are.

Make sure everyone sees the same thing

Rather than have the people in the room looking at a PowerPoint show and the people on line following along as well as they can, try hosting the whole meeting in WebEx or Lync (or whatever). This accomplishes a couple of things simultaneously:

- You can project the meeting on the wall, still projecting the same visuals. This way, whether they're in the room or not, everyone's seeing the same thing.

- You can take advantage of the chat, question and hands up features. Even if it's projected behind you, someone can point out when you have a question or comment from the field.

- Whiteboard exercises still work this way, and it's more likely you'll get quality input from the people outside the room.

One other advantage of this approach is that, even if it's only at the beginning of the meeting, the remote attendees can use their webcams to introduce themselves or just say hi.

If someone in the room has their laptop or tablet there as well, have them set it up to show the rest of the room to your remote participants.

Train yourself to include remote participants first.

If you think about the way human beings communicate, it makes perfect sense that we go to the people in the room first. It's not that we're intentionally snubbing the people on the phone (at least we hope not!) it's just that we are primarily visual creatures.

In the room you have people raising their hands for attention. You can scan the room and read their faces to get your presentation cues; speed up, slow down, what the heck were you talking about? More importantly, we tend to see someone has a question and call on them.

The problem is we can't see the faces of the people connected remotely. By the time we get around to asking them for their questions or comments the key points have been made or they're just plain tired and grumpy from waiting or trying to get a word in edgewise.

Here's one simple trick to getting better input and helping the people out in the provinces feel more included. Just start your questioning with the people connected remotely.

When it comes time for questions...or you want to get their input, simply force yourself to stop. Pause. Then ask for questions but start consciously with the people connected remotely. Maybe it's an "anyone" type question: "For those of you connected remotely, what questions do you have?"

Or, if you want to hear from a specific individual you can call on them by name. That works too.

Either way, the purpose of this is not to now exclude your in-room folks, or give preferential treatment to those who couldn't be bothered coming into the office. Instead it's to break ourselves of the habit of going always to the people sitting right in front of our faces.

Hybrid meetings will almost always be a case of "making do". The trick to making them successful is to maximize the quality of input and social interaction, while minimizing the barriers (often perceived, but just as daunting) to inclusion and garnering great ideas.

Conclusion: Now What, Smart Guy?

That great philosopher Jessica Rabbit once said, in a voice much deeper and sultrier than mine, "I'm not bad, I'm just drawn that way". Virtual meetings aren't inherently evil; they just often appear that way.

At the beginning of this book, we took the radical position that meetings, virtual or otherwise, aren't bad in and of themselves. I agree, though more often than not the evidence supports our prejudices. That doesn't mean they can't be better. The technology can be used better. You as a meeting leader, can be better.

What makes a bad meeting? It's one that wastes time, discourages good team communication, limits input, and ultimately gets in the way of getting our work done. We've tried to help you address those problems in these pages.

First, we took a look at what we want our meetings to accomplish. We've asked you to use the Meeting Assessment Form to take a good hard look at what currently works, and what doesn't.

Secondly, we looked at the limits, and maybe more importantly the possibilities, of webmeeting tools and platforms. Do you understand how they can encourage, capture and maximize your team's brainpower and engagement?

If so, we've given you planning tools to help identify those tools that can help you meet specific meeting needs. If not, quit reading this and go back to your WebEx, Lync or other account. Start poking around and learn what features it has, and how they work.

Go ahead. We'll wait.

We've discussed how the strengths or weakness of a team's meetings lie in the people on them. Participants have a responsibility to participate and contribute to the group's work. We've given you lots of tips and best practices to encourage, cajole, even coerce them into giving their best. Yes, it will take hard work and patience to break bad habits, but it can be done.

Finally, the ultimate responsibility lies with the leader. Anyone can run a virtual meeting. Leading one takes time, patience, practice and the right mindset. It starts with planning for success.

It's your task to help others be successful by creating a thoughtful, purposeful agenda and getting it to them in time to truly prepare for, and think about, the hard task of working together. We've given you the planning tools to create a reusable template. What are you going to do about that?

We've discussed best practices and techniques for leading and facilitating productive discussions and getting the best possible input to turn your meeting attendees into meeting participants. Some of them are simple, few of them are easy. They will, however, become easier with practice.

Almost everything in this book is designed to create good habits, and creating habits takes just as much repetition as breaking the old ones.

Get on it.

In the back of the book you'll find blank copies of the assessments and planning tools we've shared. Have at it.

If you have found this book helpful, and want to share it with others in your organization, go ahead. If you want more help or practice developing these skills, we'd urge you to visit us at www.GreatWebMeetings.com. There we offer white papers, articles and tools under our "Resources" section, and training classes under our "Events" and "Services" tabs.

We've done our best to help. Now it's up to you.

Are you ready to start meeting like you mean it?

Appendix

Tools and Planning Sheets

Traditional Meeting Assessment Checklist

Meeting Factor	Meets/Doesn't Meet Expectations (be specific)	Next Steps (be specific)
The meetings start on time		
The desired outcome is clearly stated at the start of each meeting		
The meetings have a detailed agenda		
Participants received the agenda in plenty of time to prepare for the meeting		
All participants have all necessary documents or information before discussion starts		
All participants clearly understand the rules for taking questions, feedback and comments		
The most important action items are handled first		
Sufficient tools like clean whiteboards, handouts and chart paper are are available		

The session leader appears in control of the participants		
All participants are solicited for input		
All participants' opinions are heard and respected		
Questions are solicited and answered to the participants' satisfaction		
All action items are clearly recapped and documented		
The objectives are met and next steps are clear		
The meeting stays on track and (more or less) on time		

Virtual Meeting Assessment Checklist

Meeting Factor	Meets/Doesn't Meet Expectations (be specific)	Next Steps (be specific)
The meetings start on time		
The desired outcome is clearly stated at the start of each meeting		
The meetings have a detailed agenda		
Participants received a the agenda in plenty of time to prepare for the meeting		
All participants have all necessary documents or information before discussion starts		
All participants clearly understand the rules for taking questions, feedback and comments		
The most important action items are handled first		
The session leader appears in control of the technology		
The session leader appears in control of the participants		
All participants are solicited for input		

All participants' opinions are heard and respected		
Questions are solicited and answered to the participants' satisfaction		
The technology functions properly (e.g., people can join the meeting with little problem or drama)		
The technology actually adds value to the process, and isn't a distraction		
All action items are clearly recapped and documented		
The objectives are met and next steps are clear		
The meeting stays on track and (more or less) on time		

Simple Meeting Agenda Template

Meeting Logistics

- Time of the meeting and when it will end
- How to test your connection in advance of the meeting
- The meeting link with password information
- A tool to enter it automatically in their calendar
- Audio information

Purpose: The purpose of the meeting is to _____

Agenda Items and Timeline: Here's what we'll do in our time together _____

Meeting Outcomes: At the end of our meeting, we will have

_____

During our time together we'll _____

and _____ so that (tell them how this will impact their work or project)

To make the most of our time together please:

1. State what they need to read or prepare to contribute
2. Describe what activities will happen during the meeting and how they will participate

In order to make the best use of everyone's time and reduce confusion, please download the following document(s) (include link to any documents or pre-work) and be prepared to _____ (Use behavior specific words)_____

About GreatWebMeetings.com

GreatWebMeetings.com is the world leader in helping develop the skills to sell, present, train and lead people using today's virtual presentation and online meeting technology.

Based in suburban Chicago, IL, we work with companies and their people around the world to overcome resistance to technology. We do this by focusing people on their real work, and using the tools to help get work done through great, and timeless, communication skills.

Visit our website at www.GreatWebMeetings.com for how scheduled classes, free resources and more. For weekly blog posts on the world of remote work, check out our blog at www.TheConnectedManager.com.

We offer standard and tailored programs in the skills remote workers need most:

- Web Presentation Basics
- Leading Effective Virtual Meetings
- How to Create and Manage Remote Teams
- Lync for Leaders
- WebEx for Leaders

Acknowledgements

I'd like to thank a lot of people for the experience, bloody noses and hard lessons that have led up to doing this book. In many ways it's an act of therapy.

There are also many people who've contributed their time by listening as I spoke through ideas, read rough drafts, sent me back to the drawing board, and talked me off various ledges. David Dalka, Lynn Sherman, Pat Ryan, and many others, thank you.

A special thanks to the indefatigable Robyn Clark for her patience, eagle eyes, and energy in the face of her own crazy existence. It's important to know what you do well, and where to find people smarter but more modest than you to do the hard work and are happy to let you shine.

Finally, thanks to the thousands of hardworking, dedicated and long-suffering middle managers I've had the pleasure of working with over the years. We get a bad rap, and treated like a punchline, but at the end of the day we are left with the responsibility of getting the work done, while not having nearly enough of the authority. This book is for you.

Made in the
USA
Lexington, KY